Jean Toomer

Jean Toomer

Selected Essays
and Literary Criticism

Edited, with an Introduction,
by Robert B. Jones

The University of Tennessee Press • Knoxville

First Edition.

The publishers gratefully acknowledge the assistance of the following people in preparing this book under most unusual circumstances: Ida Faye Jones, Dr. Jones's sister; Dr. Melvin Friedman of the University of Wisconsin at Milwaukee; and curator Patricia Willis and her staff at the American Literature Collection of the Beinecke Rare Book and Manuscript Library at Yale University.

The paper in this book meets the minimum requirements of the American National Standard for Permanence of Paper for Printed Library Materials.
♾ The binding materials have been chosen for strength and durability.

Printed on recycled paper.

Library of Congress Cataloging-in-Publication Data

Toomer, Jean, 1894-1967.
Selected Essays and Literary Criticism / by Jean Toomer; edited, with an introduction, by Robert B. Jones. — 1st ed.
p. cm.
Includes bibliographical references (p.).
ISBN 0-87049-938-6 (cloth: alk. paper)
1. Afro-Americans—Civilization. 2. Afro-Americans in literature.
I. Jones, Robert B. II. Title.
PS3539.O478A6 1996
814'.52—dc20 95-41825
CIP

Contents

Foreword

The publication of this collection of Jean Toomer's literary criticism and other essays comes at a propitious moment, and it is a major contribution to the reevaluation of Toomer's position in American intellectual and literary culture now under way. The resurgent interest in Toomer today is of a character quite different from that which established his position in the American literary canon in the 1960s and 1970s; from the essays collected here by Robert B. Jones, we can see clearly why a change was in order. Whereas *Cane,* Toomer's most important literary accomplishment, was initially "rediscovered" as a seminal text of black self-affirmation, more recent scholarship has taken more seriously (while not always accepting) Toomer's point of view that such self-affirmation was merely a step on the way to the realization of a prototypical "American" selfhood, and finally a higher realization of what he once termed the "blue man."

The changing concept of Toomer's significance coincides with a transformation in scholarly concepts of "race" and "racialism," a repudiation of essentialist assumptions that race is a natural category of identity, as well as a recognition of the importance of racialization (the enculturation of identity along "racial" lines enforced by racist domination) to American identity and thus to American writing. During his most productive years as a man of letters, Toomer made such racialization and its spiritual effects one of the main targets of his criticism. It would seem that only lately are we beginning to understand what he was about and also to recognize how thoroughly intertwined are the African American and European American literary traditions.

The current resurgence of interest in Toomer also coincides with a rise in the number of persons in the United States who consider themselves multiracial or multicultural—who, in most cases because they have parents of different races, and because they identify with both parents, question their traditional places in American racial discourse. Toomer would undoubtedly have been pleased by this. Whatever view the reader has of this phenomenon and its larger implications, it is remarkable in American cultural history; it is also inevitable that along with this phenomenon would come the publication of Jean Toomer's long-buried writings.

Robert B. Jones is one of the scholars we have to thank for the reconsideration of Toomer, and this book is one of the most important of his contributions—an important contribution, indeed, to the understanding of American literary modernism. Tragically, Professor Jones passed away after submitting the manuscript for publication and before he could respond to readers' suggestions or to new developments in Toomer scholarship; that is the reason for this Foreword.

Certain aspects of the introduction that Jones would undoubtedly have changed have been left as he wrote them. For example, Toomer's essay "The Negro Emergent" is no longer "newly discovered," as it has been cited in recent scholarship and published (incompletely) in another recent volume, a book ambitiously entitled *A Jean Toomer Reader,* edited by Frederik L. Rusch and published by Oxford University Press. That book contains little of Toomer's literary criticism. The only pieces that appear in it as well as in this book are "Negro Psychology in *The Emperor Jones*" and "The Negro Emergent" (from which an important paragraph was unaccountably deleted in Rusch's *Reader*). Their reappearance here is fully justified by the benefits to be had by reading them in the context of Toomer's other important essays. Furthermore, this edition of Toomer's little-known prose work has the advantage of presenting almost exclusively uncut texts—an extremely important point, considering the iconoclasm of Toomer's ideas and the ease with which, quoted piecemeal or published with omissions, they can be made to support positions greatly at variance with the author's own—positions that were, as a rule, subtle and complex.

This newly published work, as Robert Jones's introduction emphasizes, clearly positions Toomer primarily in a different sector of the American literary field than that to which he has usually been assigned. However, recent discoveries and scholarship also show that the question of whether Toomer belonged to the Lost Generation or to the Negro Renaissance—a question first asked by S. P. Fullinwider—is itself somewhat misleading. Although Toomer did not think of himself as a "New Negro," correspondence between Alain Locke, Georgia Douglas Johnson, and Jean Toomer reveals that Toomer did, in fact, participate in—and even instigate—literary activities of so-called New Negroes in Washington, D.C., and then New York before, during, and after the writing of *Cane*; Alain Locke was one of his first literary advisors, and Toomer knew well many of the contributors to *The New Negro.* Indeed, he converted several of them to the Gurdjieffian spiritual program in the mid-1920s. This is not to say that he fits comfortably within the Harlem Renaissance designation. But neither did many of the other New Negroes.

Increasingly, scholars are recognizing the large differences between African American modernists and their varied relations to other, nonblack writers. The divisions between them often corresponded with divisions in the American literary field generally, not only on issues of race but also in terms of philosophy, style, and literary form. *The New Negro* itself, in which Alain Locke included Toomer's work without permission, is a self-divided text representing a range of positions from black cultural nationalism and pan-Africanism to a sort of "amalgamationism" not all that different from Toomer's. Georgia Douglas Johnson's poem "The Riddle," for example, expresses a Toomeresque vision of a "new race"—both black *and* white—that undoubtedly owes something to the meetings Toomer conducted on this subject at Johnson's home in the early 1920s, and to which he invited Alain Locke. Nonetheless, clearly Toomer did not choose to affiliate *primarily* with the black literary community; by the time *Cane* appeared, he did not accept the racial designation American culture insisted on assigning him. Frustration at making his racial position understood helped lead Toomer to abandon literature, convinced that literary ambitions corrupted the search for a fully human identity and equally convinced of the inadequacy of language to express truth. Hence, he turned to a series of religious programs in the attempt to transcend the society in which he was enveloped. One of the constants in all of this was the figure of Walt Whitman, in whom Toomer first began to find his poetic voice (his "American" voice), whom A. R. Orage presented as the great American prophet of "cosmic consciousness," and to whose natal religious denomination—the Society of Friends—Toomer would finally turn.

But if Toomer fits the Harlem Renaissance designation uncomfortably at best, the term "Lost Generation" can be equally misleading when applied to him, since it has been defined primarily in relation to writers such as Ezra Pound, T. S. Eliot, Ernest Hemingway, and F. Scott Fitzgerald. Toomer was affiliated with a quite different circle of "white" authors who believed in "the promise of America"—an America, that is, conceived along new lines. Cultural nationalists of a somewhat romantic sort, they prophesied an indigenous American spiritual ripening that would replenish the modern wasteland, and they tended toward mysticism. They included Waldo Frank, Paul Rosenfeld, Sherwood Anderson, Gorham Munson, Alfred Stieglitz, Margaret Naumburg, and other like-minded writers. Their differences with Eliot and Pound were at least as great as those between the self-identified New Negro authors and Jean Toomer throughout the late 1910s and early to mid-1920s. In *Our America,* for example, Waldo Frank imagined a soldier returning from World War I and coming to quite different conclusions from Hemingway's sensitive veterans. Although Frank's soldier sees the myths and lies of the dominant culture for what they are, "He slaps his thigh and finds that only he is sound. . . . Give him time. He is the bringer of a new religion, he is the maker of multitudes." New Negroes could well have re-imagined Frank's soldier as black, in a way they could not have imagined Hemingway's.

Indeed, Toomer's circle and others connected to it—including editors and contributors to such journals as the *Liberator* (to which Toomer submitted some of his earliest work from *Cane,* and which Claude McKay helped edit), the *New Republic,* and the *Nation*—had close and complex relations with the Harlem Renaissance. Along with the *Crisis, Opportunity,* and the *Messenger*—"Negro" magazines to which Toomer acquaintances from Waldo Frank to the Provincetown group contributed—Toomer's circle played an important role in the Harlem Renaissance's gestation and promotion. The "high modernists" (as Toomer's critical essays here reveal) they regarded as intelligent but shallow aesthetes, lacking in substance and spirit, the very qualities they felt New Negro writing provided in drawing on its own "indigenous" American roots. Their disappearance from traditional accounts of modernism is partly responsible for the popular sense of a large gap between a monolithic Anglo-American modernism and the Harlem Renaissance, a gap that only reaffirms the forms of American racial discourse that Jean Toomer, more intently than anyone else of his era or ours, refused to accept.

To make a choice, then, between Harlem Renaissance and Lost Generation as a label for Toomer will not quite do. The New Negro movement itself was closely linked to the concepts promoted in *The Seven Arts,* which Frank and Rosenfeld helped edit, which published Claude McKay's first "American" poems, and which Alain Locke followed enthusiastically on the verge of the twenties. Like the intertextual relations between "black-authored" and "white-authored" literary works, the relationships between "black" and "white" intellectuals in New York in the 1910s and 1920s, both personally and intellectually, were far more fluid and complex—and productive—than American scholarship has acknowledged. The essays collected here enhance such acknowledgment considerably, with implications for the transformation of our understanding of American modernism as well as the interracial cultural history of the United States. Certainly, such was Robert Jones's large and generous aim in creating this important book.

George Hutchinson
The University of Tennessee
Knoxville

Introduction

Jean Toomer, Lost Generation or Harlem Renaissance? This question underscores Toomer's unique and controversial position in the history of American and African American literature. For while *Cane* remains his masterwork and signal accomplishment, his subsequent works reveal ideas and critiques commonly associated with the Lost Generation. In a review of a collection of Toomer's unpublished writings, *The Wayward and the Seeking,* novelist and critic Alice Walker writes:

> It will no doubt be hard, if not impossible, for lovers of *Cane* to read *The Wayward and the Seeking* (the title is from one of Toomer's poems) without feelings of disappointment and loss. Disappointment because the man who wrote so piercingly of "Negro" life in *Cane* chose to live his life as a white man, while Hughes, Hurston, Du Bois and other black writers were celebrating the blackness in themselves as well as in their works. Loss because it appears this choice undermined Toomer's moral judgement: There were things in American life and in his own that he simply refused to see.[1]

Walker's comments represent a popular school of thought in Jean Toomer criticism that interprets his life and works after *Cane* in terms of racial denial. This school believes that writers of African American heritage should focus exclusively on racial themes and subjects; that Toomer's racial idealism was a clever ruse to deny his heritage; and that his "raceless" writings (the majority of his canon) should be banished into obscurity. To my mind, however, Toomer's significance must ultimately be evaluated in light of his contributions to both African American *and* American literature. And as responsible critics we must seek to form the canon rather than dismiss it. Specifically, we must examine the intricate network of intertextual relations between *Cane* and the rest of the oeuvre; the relationship (or nonrelationship) between Toomer and his contemporaries of the 1920s; and the relationship between Toomer and history itself. In this way, a detailed portrait of the artist, not just a silhouette, emerges.

Like T. S. Eliot, F. Scott Fitzgerald, and Ernest Hemingway, Toomer dissociated himself from the materialism engendered by postwar prosperity, and moralized on the modern world as a wasteland; and like Lewis Mumford, Waldo Frank, and Van Wyck Brooks, he wrote essays critical of the social and cultural climate of the twenties. It is a commonly held belief that Toomer's literary artistry devolved into moral pronouncements after the publication of *Cane,* owing to the influence of Gurdjieffian philosophy. Yet his position as moral spokesman for the Lost Generation did not derive from Gurdjieff; rather it derived from his own sense of indignation over the direction the country was going. Thus, if the writings after *Cane* lack rhythms, rhapsodies, and refrains, it is because he shifted his emphasis from Symbolism to social idealism. In this context, I beg to differ with Walker's assessment of Toomer's lapse in "moral judgement," his refusal to see the social realities around him; rather, he saw postwar America primarily through the lens of the Lost Generation.

The Lost Generation defines a group of writers, artists, and intellectuals of the 1920s who felt that traditional values had been lost to them as a result of the war and the nature of the modern world. According to Malcolm Cowley, "The generation belonged to a period of transition from values already fixed to values that had to be created . . . they were seceding from the old and yet could adhere to nothing new. . . . It was not by accident that their early books were almost all nostalgic, full of the wish to recapture some remembered thing."[2] What they all held in common was a rejection of the values of postwar America. And many of them, like Hart Crane, Waldo Frank, Gorham Munson, Zona Gale, Paul Rosenfeld, Margery Latimer, and Jean Toomer, turned to idealist metaphysics and Gurdjieffian philosophy, as if to counter the materialism of the age with mysticism and philosophy. Toomer's sense of rejection is manifested not only in his philosophical idealism, but also in his literary works, as Warren French demonstrates in his comparative analysis of *Cane* and Eliot's *The Waste Land,* as Thomas A. Gullason notes in his essay on the American short story in the 1920s, and as I have illustrated in an intertextual study of Toomer's *Lost and Dominant* and *The Waste Land.*[3] Thus, while some critics will censure Toomer for not assimilating into the Harlem Renaissance, others will appreciate the new and important perspectives his social and cultural critiques provide on the intellectual and historical milieu of his time.

Shortly after the publication of *Cane* in October of 1923, Toomer joined an informal brotherhood of writers, intellectuals, and critics—a circle that included Waldo Frank, Gorham Munson, Alfred Kreymborg, Allen Tate, Van Wyck Brooks, Matthew Josephson, and Kenneth Burke. Through this circle he also developed literary liaisons with Paul Rosenfeld, Alfred Stieglitz, Sherwood Anderson, and Hart Crane. They all shared in a disregard for postwar materialism, industrialism, and commercialism, and actively sought to refocus America's values, and they attempted to affirm uniquely American ethics and aesthetics in their writings. There was a high level of literary interaction, as they publicized and promoted each other's works. Waldo Frank, associate editor of *The Seven Arts,* wrote the Foreword to *Cane*; Toomer reviewed Gorham Munson's *Waldo Frank: A Study* in *S4N*; Munson and Toomer served together on the editorial board of *S4N*; Munson included a chapter on Toomer in his *Destinations: A Canvass of American Literature Since 1900*; Munson (along with Matthew Josephson and Kenneth Burke) edited *Secession*; *Broom* associate editor Matthew Josephson praised *Cane* as a "great American novel"; Toomer corresponded with Kenneth Burke and reviewed his *The White Oxen* in the *Little Review*; *Broom* associate editor Malcolm Cowley included Toomer in his "literary odyssey of the 1920s," *Exile's Return*; Paul Rosenfeld's *Men Seen: Twenty Four Modern Authors* contains a chapter on Toomer; Toomer wrote an unpublished review of Rosenfeld's *Port of New York*; Rosenfeld appears as a roman à clef character in Toomer's novella *York Beach*; Rosenfeld dedicated his book *An Hour with American Music* to Jean Toomer; Toomer and Sherwood Anderson praised each other's work in their correspondence; *Camera Work* editor Alfred Stieglitz and his wife, Georgia O'Keeffe, often invited Toomer to their Lake George home in New York; Toomer praised Stieglitz as an artist in *America and Alfred Stieglitz: A Collective Portrait,* edited by Waldo Frank, Lewis Mumford, Dorothy Norman, Harold Rugg, and Paul Rosenfeld; in a letter to Alfred Stieglitz, Hart Crane described his "little handful" of best friends as comprising Waldo Frank, Margaret Naumburg, Gorham Munson, and Jean Toomer; it was Crane who introduced Toomer's writings to Allen Tate; and Toomer sent Crane a signed copy of *Cane*: "For Hart, instrument of the highest beauty, whose art, four-conscinal, rich in symbols and ecstasy, is great—whose touch, deep and warm, is a sheer illumination."[4] "Little Magazines" also greatly contributed to Toomer's literary prominence during the 1920s. His first installments of *Cane* were published in *Broom, Nomad,* the *Little Review,* the *Liberator, Double Dealer, Prairie,* and *S4N*; and he published literary essays and reviews in *Dial, Broom,* the *Little Review, S4N,* the British little magazine called the *Adelphi,* and the French little magazine *Bifur.*

The present volume constitutes a collection of primary source materials and criticism by Jean Toomer, illustrating the range of his thinking from 1921 to 1949. Many of these essays are published here for the first time, while others have been resurrected from the pages of little magazines of the 1920s. Individually and collectively, these essays provide a variety of new perspectives on Toomer beyond his masterwork, *Cane.*

The literary criticism and reviews demonstrate not only Toomer's acumen as a literary critic, but his literary aesthetics as well. The first two essays, both written in 1921, disclose aspects of Toomer's pre-*Cane* literary aesthetics. In his review of "The Art of Poetry," he demonstrates his thorough knowledge of Imagism and its "art for art's sake" aestheticism.[5] Indeed, as early as 1920, he embraced Imagist aesthetics as having literary tenets consistent with his own. "Their insistence on fresh vision and on the perfect clean economical line was just what I had been looking for. I began feeling that I had in my hands the tools for my own creation."[6] Notwithstanding his high regard for Imagist technical precision and formal mastery, he criticizes Imagist poetry as out of touch with its Western literary tradition, with "the mighty voices of the past": "We of the Western world, whose thoughts have been shaped and moulded by the poets from Plato (Goethe, Ibsen, etc.) to Whitman suddenly roll on our backs with our faces towards China and the Chinese. Charmed by their pictorial, suggestive loveliness we no longer hear the mighty voices of the past." Thus, Toomer implies that poetry should serve a moral as well as an aesthetic function.

Although brief, "Negro Psychology in *The Emperor Jones*" manifests Toomer's early interest in the psychology of character; further, it suggests an intertextual link between Eugene O'Neill's play and Toomer's play *Kabnis,* which was rewritten as Part Three of *Cane.* Like O'Neill, Toomer represents the psychology of racial fear in the central character, and Kabnis, like Brutus Jones, confronts his racial past as he regresses through individual memory to the racial unconscious.

"Waldo Frank's *Holiday*" and "The South in Literature" both analyze Waldo Frank's novel *Holiday,* although from different perspectives. Published in 1923, Frank's *Holiday,* like *Cane,* portrays the life and culture of African Americans in the rural South in the early 1920s. It is generally known that Toomer lived in rural Sparta, Georgia, for two months during the fall of 1921, while serving as interim headmaster of the Sparta Agricultural and Industrial Institute and writing *Cane.* Few people know, however, that a year later he returned South with Waldo Frank to recapture the moments he had lived through during the previous year. Frank, too, had visited the South a year earlier, living in Tuskegee, Alabama, and in New Orleans, Louisiana. In August of 1922, fired by the anticipation of their new journey together, Toomer wrote to Frank: "I cannot think of myself as being separated from you in the dual task of creating an American literature, and of developing a public, however large or small, capable of responding to our creations. Those who read and know me should read and know you."[7] A month later, they traveled to Spartanburg, South Carolina. Like Toomer, Frank was olive-complexioned, and they lived as African Americans among African Americans for a week. And when they returned home—Toomer to Washington and Frank to New York—the two writers commented on each other's drafts of *Cane* and *Holiday* over the next several months. In "Waldo Frank's *Holiday*" Toomer concentrates on "the unspoken consciousness" as a major element of Frank's literary aesthetic; "The South in Literature," however, is important not only for its analyses of *Holiday,* but also more for its perspectives on *Cane.* Here, for the first time, Toomer provides an extended critical analysis of his own masterwork. Particularly illuminating are the author's comments on *Kabnis.*

His review of Zona Gale's *Faint Perfume* suggests that he valued emotion and feeling in literature, yet found it curiously lacking in Gale's novel. A best-seller in 1923, *Faint Perfume* is the story of a young female writer, Leda Perrin, who returns home to Prospect (Portage, Wisconsin) from New York to reorient her life. Like her Pulitzer Prize–winning novel *Miss Lula Bett* (1920), it is a family story in the local-color tradition. Yet Toomer describes the book as "emotionally thin and curiously without body," and he characterizes Leda Perrin as "a mild and somewhat passive sensitivity in contact with life's innocuous commonplaces." Several years later, Gale and Toomer belonged to the same Gurdjieff group, and it was she who indirectly introduced Toomer to his first wife, Margery Latimer. Both Gale and Latimer were natives of Portage, Wisconsin, and Gale became a dominant force in Latimer's life. In January of 1926, Gale persuaded Latimer to attend a lecture and demonstration on Gurdjieffian philosophy; later they began regularly attending these meetings. Coincidentally, Toomer was also attending the same meetings, although he did not know Latimer at the time. In May of 1931, Latimer joined Toomer's Gurdjieff group, having been favorably impressed by his book of aphorisms, *Essentials.* After a courtship lasting several months, they were married in October of 1931.

"Open Letter to Gorham Munson," a response to Munson's essay "The Mechanics for a Literary 'Secession,'" provides some important perspectives on how history influenced the aesthetic thinking of Toomer and his contemporaries. In 1922, *S4N* editor Norman Fitts invited Munson, the editor of *Secession,* to write a manifesto essay descriptive of contemporary aesthetics. In "The Mechanics for a Literary 'Secession,'" Munson proposed that modern America accept the machine as a necessary evil, coexisting in a dialectical tension with art and aesthetics. Indeed, he suggests that modern writers incorporate their ideas on the sterility and materialism of the age into the creation of a new modern literature, as Pound had done in *Hugh Selwyn Mauberly,* Eliot in *The Waste Land,* Fitzgerald in *The Great Gatsby,* and Hemingway in *The Sun Also Rises.* In metaphors indicating materialism as a modern disease, he advocates that modern literature function as an antibody against industrialism, pragmatism, and rationalism, thereby asserting the viability of literature against the ravages of the machine. When Munson's essay appeared in the November 1922 issue of *S4N,* Toomer, who served on its editorial board, wrote a response, in which he agrees with Munson's notion of forging a new national literature, and even admits to his own unconscious complicity in the ascendancy of the machine: "I had been in every powerhouse in the city years before I dragged myself into the Corcoran Gallery. And I neglected the 'poetry of the people' for such things as motorcycle motors, dynamos and generators. The first thing I made from cardboard was a battleship. There is not a statue in Washington with the living beauty of line and balance of certain Pierce-Arrow cars. And the National Museum looks mouldy besides any automobile show window." Toomer nevertheless criticizes Munson's manifesto for reinstating the dialectics of man and nature, self and world, form and content:

> Briefly stated, [Munson's] program is as follows: There are now three factors in the spiritual life of man: man himself, Nature, and the Machine. The machine, when first introduced, destroyed the balance which man had achieved with nature, and the old art of adjustment gave way to a disjointed art. To date, the art of maladjustment has tried to meet man's spiritual conflicts in two ways: first, by a total rejection of the Machine, that is, by a back-to nature program; second, by accepting the Machine as a necessary evil and erecting against it certain counter forms. The former of these has been demonstrated to be impotent. The latter, despite the body of first-rate literature that it has produced, may in reality resolve into nothing more vital than a compromise, a dualism, 'an antagonism specifically

similar to that between man and nature promulgated by the puritans.' If this be true, then it follows that man must override this dualism, that he must evolve a creative amalgam of himself, Nature, and the Machine.

"Notations on *The Captain's Doll*" registers Toomer's familiarity with the writings of D. H. Lawrence. Lawrence's short novels *The Captain's Doll, The Fox,* and *The Ladybird* were written in 1921 and collectively published as *The Ladybird* in England, and as *The Captain's Doll* in America in 1923. In his review, Toomer criticizes Lawrence for using symbols ineffectively to advance the action, for failing to employ effective character development, and for creating too solemn a tone in works that convey, in his words, "a serious sense of the unusual." Notwithstanding his negative review, Toomer was impressed by Lawrence's exploration of mystical conceptions of personal relationships, conceptions Toomer himself explores in "Withered Skin of Berries" (1922), *Natalie Mann* (1922), and *Eight Day World* (1929), as well as in *Cane.*

One of the finest essays in this volume is "The Critic of Waldo Frank: Criticism, An Art Form," a cogent examination of Gorham Munson's *Waldo Frank: A Study* (1923). Here Toomer demonstrates his considerable knowledge of Frank's major novels—*The Unwelcome Man* (1917), *The Dark Mother* (1920), *Rahab* (1922), and *City Block* (1922)—in his commentaries on aesthetics, American cultural criticism, and form in the American novel. Frank's novels, marked by mysticism, poetic style, and introspective analysis, represent fictional applications of his own philosophy, a mixture of spiritual prophecy, psychoanalysis, and social criticism on the dilemma of modern man. As Toomer shows, the basis of Frank's social and cultural criticism, however, is contained in *Our America* (1919), a treatise that traces America's materialism and moral bankruptcy back to the Puritans and pioneers, who sublimated their feelings, emotions, and desires into industry, technology, and utilitarian ethics. In this way, Frank argues, they devalued consciousness, art, and aesthetics, like their counterparts of the 1920s. In obvious agreement with Frank's thesis and impressed by Munson's range and depth as a literary critic, Toomer praises the book as "an art product in the critical form."

While most critics and admirers of Toomer are aware of his many literary relationships of the 1920s, few are aware of his friendship with literary critic and philosopher Kenneth Burke, author of *Counter-Statement* (1931), *The Philosophy of Literary Form* (1941), and *A Grammar of Motives* (1945). Burke also wrote several works of fiction, including *The White Oxen* (1924), the subject of Toomer's "Oxen Cart and Warfare."

Toomer and Burke corresponded throughout the early 1920s; when Toomer's lukewarm review appeared in *The Little Review,* Burke wrote to him and acknowledged the wisdom of his criticisms:

> All told, I believe now that your article was better than it will ever get credit for . . . I do wish, as a matter of objective interest, that you had gone into the matter of conflicts more at length and more in general . . . I sometimes wonder whether your distinction might not have been drawn differently; and we might situate the failure of my stories in the fact that they deal with an ethical conflict which has not been resolved into an artistic unity. I never found the creative symbol, the emotional unit which would include logical opposites. . . . Out of it all I arrived, sullenly yet without choice, at the feeling that I can write nothing but an objective novel. I am, in other words, exactly at that point at which I stood when writing the story of *The White Oxen.*[8]

During the same year, 1924, Toomer reviewed the work of another member of his circle, Paul Rosenfeld, a New York music, art, and literary critic. Rosenfeld's most important contributions to American literary criticism are *Port of New York* (1924), a collection of essays on fourteen artists, writers, composers, and educators of the 1920s (including Van Wyck Brooks, Carl Sandburg, William Carlos Williams, Margaret Naumburg, John Marin, Sherwood Anderson, Georgia O'Keeffe, Randolph Bourne, and Alfred Stieglitz), and *Men Seen: Twenty Four Modern Authors* (1925). It is the earlier work that is the subject of Toomer's "Paul Rosenfeld in Port," an essay that uses Van Wyck Brooks's concept of "Puritan dividedness" to elucidate Rosenfeld's thinking:

> Van Wyck Brooks gave the idea of "Puritan dividedness" to America, and particularly to his literary stratum. It was by means of this idea, with its emphasis on milieu rather than on the individual, its call for soil and cultural interpenetration, its formula of dualism and the correlative formula of oneness, its earthiness, emotional direction, sensuosity, anti-intellection, its humanity and Americanism; it was by means of this idea that Brooks' literary stratum coalesced and grew articulate. . . . On the plane of cultural speculation, "Puritan dividedness" opened desirable vistas in America for Mr. Rosenfeld.

The final essay of the literary criticism and reviews is taken from "The Psychology and Craft of Writing," the first in a series of eight lectures Toomer projected but never completed. Though incomplete, this essay outlines his "program for writing"—his attempts to essentialize and spiritualize experience in the process of literary creation:

> In writing I aim to do two main things. One. To essentialize experience. To essentialize is to strip a thing of its nonessentials and to experience the concentrated kernel of the thing. Two. To spiritualize experience. To spiritualize is to have one's psyche or spirit engage in a process similar to that of the body when it digests and assimilates food. To spiritualize is to digest, assimilate, up-grade, and form the materials of experience—in fine, to form oneself. It is the direct opposite of sensualization, and of mechanization. It has to do with intensifying and vivifying both the writer and the reader.

In addition to the literary criticism and reviews, there are also cultural and social essays on American society in the 1920s. A newly discovered essay, "The Negro Emergent," ranks with Alain Locke's *The New Negro* as a landmark in the history of African American cultural criticism. Written in 1924, a year before Locke's *The New Negro: An Interpretation,* Toomer's essay defines the spiritual transformation of black Americans in the 1920s, as well as the social, cultural, and racial parameters of the Harlem Renaissance. According to Locke, black Americans experienced "a spiritual Coming of Age" in the 1920s: "The mind of the Negro seems suddenly to have slipped from under the tyranny of social intimidation and to be shaking off the psychology of imitation and implied inferiority. By shedding the old chrysalis of the Negro problem we are achieving something like a spiritual emancipation. . . . The American mind must reckon with a fundamentally changed Negro."[9] Toomer similarly argues that "an impulse is at work . . . detaching the essential Negro from the social crust":

> Generally, it may be said that the Negro is emergent from a crust, a false personality, a compound of beliefs, habits, attitudes, and emotional reactions superimposed upon him by external circumstances. . . . The Negro has found his roots. He is in fruitful contact with his ancestry. He partakes of an uninterrupted stream of energy. He is moved by the vital determinants of racial heritage. And something of their spirit now lives within him. He is about to harvest whatever the past has stored, good and evil. He is about to be released from an unconscious and negative concern with it.

In "The Crock of Problems" Toomer enumerates the facts of his own racial ancestry, as well as his controversial views on racial and democratic idealism: "I am at once no one of the races and I am all of them. I belong to no one of them and I belong to all. I am, in a strict racial sense, a member of a new race. This new race, of which I happen to be one of the first articulate members, is now forming. . . . Heredity and environment will combine to produce a race which will be at once interracial and unique. It may be the turning point for the return of mankind, now divided into hostile races, to one unified race. . . . In so far as race and nationality are concerned, I wish to be known as an American." "Race Problems and Modern Society" is a carefully researched study in which sociology, psychology, global and American history, cultural criticism, and literary criticism are employed to analyze the sources of racial conflict in modern America. Toomer blames America's "acquisitive urge," as evidenced in its economic and political system, for modern race problems. And again he examines the evolution of "The New Negro" in the postwar decade:

> The World War and its consequences gave a decided turn to the racial situation within the Negro group . . . a number of factors, among which are greater pressure from without, increased organization and articulateness within the group, and, as a result of the World War, a deeper seated disillusion as regards the promises of the dominant white American—these together with other factors, have caused an intensification of Negro race consciousness. . . . From the point of view of deliberate intention, it would seem that the New Negro is much more Negro and much less American than was the old Negro of fifty years ago.

In addition to the essays on race, others provide new perspectives on the Lost Generation. These latter essays develop the thesis that postwar prosperity stifled American culture, placed an undue emphasis on material values, and neglected the aesthetic and spiritual dimensions of American life. Originally published in French, in the French little magazine *Bifur*, "Lettre D'Amerique" ("Letter from America") appears here in English for the first time. In this essay on the election of Herbert Hoover in 1929, Toomer interprets the social and cultural implications of Hoover's presidency in light of the rise of the cult of business, the psychology of the American businessman, and the diminished emphasis on aesthetics and social idealism. According to Toomer, Hoover was

> . . . the very symbol of business, of efficiency, of prohibition, and of Protestantism. He represents a pragmatic type, competent, yet stripped of sensitivity and imagination. He confirms that we have definitely abandoned the era of social idealism. . . . We no longer need trouble

> ourselves with dreams, with feelings, with aspirations—all positive ideals but without material advantage. . . . There was a time when America was the proud champion of social idealism. It was a country—and we were a people—of independence, equality, and liberty. At that time these were not vain slogans. We were a growing people, a people of the present and the future. This has changed. America is now a country of business, and we are a country of businessmen.

Published in May of 1929, just six months before the disastrous stock market crash, this essay remains uncannily prophetic in its vision of the tragic end of an era.

"Opinions on the Questions of the *Cahiers de l'Etoile*" is similarly a cultural critique with a Franco-American connection. When the editor of the French journal *Cahiers de l'Etoile* requested Toomer's views on the contemporary American scene, he presented his responses in an interview format. As in "Letter from America," he is especially critical of the cult of business; but he also articulates the anxieties of the Lost Generation. In response to a question on the feeling of unrest in the 1920s and how it affected creative achievement, he replied: "It is, I think, both a help and a hindrance. It is unfortunate because in the midst of it the artist is likely to be distracted and torn beyond the possibility of significant achievement. He finds comparatively nothing ready for his hand to use: no creative traditions, no energizing symbols, no satisfactory forms. He has no certainty of response from others, for he cannot assume that his forms and values, views and beliefs, are understood and affirmed (or denied) by his audience."

In "The Hill," "A New Force for Co-Operation," and "Why I Entered the Gurdjieff Work," Toomer provides some personal answers to the problems of the twenties. A sensitive tribute to renowned American photographer Alfred Stieglitz, "The Hill" appeared in *America and Alfred Stieglitz: A Collective Portrait* in 1934. In addition to Toomer's essay, this book contains contributions by Waldo Frank, Lewis Mumford, Paul Rosenfeld, William Carlos Williams, Sherwood Anderson, and Gertrude Stein. "The Hill," the Lake George (New York) home of Stieglitz and his wife, artist Georgia O'Keeffe, symbolizes a retreat from the urban wasteland; moreover, Toomer uses the natural landscape of the farm to symbolize Stieglitz's natural affinity with the American landscape, as well as his austere asceticism.

> At The Hill the windows are uncurtained. Each window is all window. The outside can look in, the Lake George landscape, near by trees, an

> old red barn, floating clouds. The house rests upon its earth, inviting this part of the American landscape to enter. And the countryside does enter, and something of the great earth, and something, I feel, of the great world.
>
> What is of equal importance, the inside can look out—and this, particularly, is Stieglitz. The inside looking out unhindered, the human spirit being, with a permanent intensity to perceive, feel, and know the world which it inhabits, to give a sheer record of experience.

"The Hill" is Toomer's voice of the thunder over the wasteland, a positive answer to the pessimistic loathing of the modern age.

Toomer also embraced spiritual and social idealism as a reaction against the materialism of the era; for him, Gurdjieffian idealism provided an answer to the angst of modernity. In this context, we are able to understand Toomer's millenarianism, his hope for a new American society, as seen in his long poem *The Blue Meridian,* in his utopian political allegories "Monrovia" and "Winter on Earth," and in his essay "A New Force for Co-Operation." Published in England in 1934, "A New Force for Co-Operation" sets forth an idealistic agenda for social change: "Only a new vital religion," writes Toomer, "will evoke from us a new force for co-operation, conscience, the transforming powers of human nature. A world-religion complete enough to include all peoples, true enough . . . to bind us together by the realisation of our common condition and our common goal, to move us towards that goal with faith and nobility and a sense of a great purpose which unites us."

"Why I Entered the Gurdjieff Work" is excerpted from "The Second River," one of Toomer's several autobiographies. Chronicling his spiritual development and his decision to become a spiritual reformer, "The Second River" outlines Toomer's first encounter with Gurdjieff and his philosophy in New York in 1923. In the excerpt selected for inclusion here, he details the design of Gurdjieff's "system," with its demonstrations of gymnastic exercises, its deeply moving music, its sacred dances, and its idealist philosophy of higher consciousness.

The essays on Quaker religious philosophy reveal a conspicuous shift away from social to religious idealism, although aspects of his social vision remain in his commentaries on the cruelty and indifference of humanity, the genocide of European Jews by the Nazis, and the Second World War. In 1936 Toomer and his second wife, Marjorie Content, moved to Doylestown, Pennsylvania, and in 1938 they began attending meetings of the Religious Society of Friends. During his apprenticeship with the Friends Society, he immersed himself in Quaker philosophy and wrote numerous essays on George Fox and Quakerism; and in 1940 he and Marjorie joined the Society of Friends. Toomer was an active Quaker for more than fifteen years, serving on committees, lecturing on Quakerism, and publishing essays in the Quaker journal, *Friends Intelligencer.*

"Why I Joined the Society of Friends" discloses Quaker religious philosophy to be a continuation of Toomer's perennial devotion to the personal and social possibilities of idealism and mysticism: "Quakers assembled, I had been told, for silent prayer and waited for the spirit to move them. This appealed to me because I practiced [transcendental] meditation. . . . Prior to coming in contact with Friends I had been convinced that God is both immanent and transcendent, and that the purpose of man's life is to grow up to God; that within man there is a wonderful power that can transform him, lift him into new birth; that we have it in us to rise to a life wherein brotherhood is manifest and war impossible." He similarly reveals the link between his earlier forms of idealism and Quaker religious idealism in "The Message of Quakerism": "Quakerism is not unique in proclaiming that something of God is in man. Hinduism proclaims the same. . . . The Catholic mystics made the same discovery."

Delivered at the Arch Meeting House in Philadelphia in 1949, "The Flavor of Man," Toomer's 1949 William Penn keynote address and the last major essay he wrote before his death, remains a testament to his enduring faith in the possibilities of the spirit, blending social with religious idealism and Neoplatonism with Quakerism. In this address he declares: "We must acknowledge that the world of darkness is potent and, at the present time, ominous; but it is not the only possible world. There is another Being behind and above our ordinary persons. There is another world behind and above our ordinary world. We must renew the vision of that other world." After 1950 Toomer produced no literary works and only two religious essays, "Something More" and "Blessing and Curse," although he continued to offer workshops on Gurdjieffian philosophy in Doylestown until plagued by ill health in 1957. After several years of invalidism—he was in and out of nursing homes and crippled by arthritis—he died in Doylestown in 1967.

As a writer and literary critic, Toomer conceived of himself as participating in the creation of a new and uniquely American literature. In his now famous letter to James Weldon Johnson, he writes: "My view of this country sees it composed of people who primarily are Americans, who secondarily are of various stocks or mixed stocks. . . . As regards art I particularly hold this view. I see our art and literature as primarily American art and literature."[10] As a cultural critic, Toomer interpreted both the Lost Generation and the Harlem Renaissance: in the tradition of Van Wyck Brooks's *America's Coming-of-Age,* Waldo Frank's *Our America,* and William Carlos Williams's *In the American Grain,* he argued that America's postwar culture placed inordinate emphases on material values, to the detriment of aesthetic and moral ones; and in the tradition of Alain Locke's *The New Negro: An Interpretation,* he defined the coming-of-age of black Americans in the 1920s. As a social critic, he condemned America's political and economic system as responsible for racism in the 1920s; and as a social visionary, he attempted to reform America into a country of the spirit, governed by the principles of racial and democratic idealism. In his last essays, as a religious writer and thinker, he continued his constant devotion to the possibilities of the spirit to create harmony and peace within the self and in society. In sum, these essays provide elucidating glimpses into the literary and cultural climate of the 1920s, into the mind of Jean Toomer, and into the history of the American experience.

Notes

1. Alice Walker, "The Divided Life of Jean Toomer," *New York Times Book Review* 85 (July 13, 1980): 11.
2. Malcolm Cowley, *Exile's Return: A Literary Odyssey of the 1920's* (New York: The Viking Press, 1951), 9.
3. See Warren French, "Afternote," The Twenties: Fiction, Poetry, Drama, ed. Warren French (Deland, Florida: Everett/Edwards, 1975), 325–33; Thomas A. Gullason, "The 'Lesser Renaissance': The American Short Story in the 1920's." *The American Short Story, 1900–1945: A Critical History,* ed. Philip Stevick (Boston: Twayne, 1984), 99–100; Robert B. Jones, "Jean Toomer's Lost and Dominant: Landscape of the Modern Waste Land," *Studies in American Fiction* 18 (Spring 1990): 77–86.
4. Thomas S. W. Lewis, ed. *Letters of Hart Crane and His Family* (New York: Columbia University Press, 1974), 215–16.
5. See Richard Aldington, "The Art of Poetry," *Dial* 69 (July–Dec. 1920): 166–80.
6. Darwin Turner, ed., *The Wayward and the Seeking: A Collection of Writings by Jean Toomer* (Washington, D.C.: Howard University Press, 1980), 120.
7. Jean Toomer, letter to Waldo Frank, dated Aug. 2, 1922. Box 3, Folder 6, the Jean Toomer Collection, Beinecke Rare Book and Research Library, Yale University, New Haven, Connecticut.
8. Kenneth Burke, Letter to Jean Toomer dated Feb. 26, 1925. Box 1,

Folder 7, the Jean Toomer Collection, Beinecke Rare Book and Manuscript Library, Yale University, New Haven, Connecticut.

9. Alain Locke, ed., *The New Negro: An Interpretation* (New York: Albert and Charles Boni, 1925), 4.
10. Jean Toomer, Letter to James Weldon Johnson dated July 11, 1930. Box 5, Folder 3, the Jean Toomer Collection, Beinecke Rare Book and Manuscript Library, Yale University, New Haven, Connecticut.

Literary Criticism and Reviews

Review of Richard Aldington's "The Art of Poetry"

I

R[ichard] A[ldington] begins by asking what is the purpose of poetry in modern life. "Obviously, the purpose is not ethical," says [Aldington]. Perhaps the best poetry of all times has been non-moral, in the sense in which we now use the term "moral." Teachers and preachers have instinctively utilized the schools and the pulpits for their purposes and left art to the artists. That is to say, those who would have life lived according to their own narrow precepts have, by their own temperaments and limitations, been forced into a mode of expression as narrow and as limited as they themselves are. Art, which embraces all life, and whose noblest function it is to expand, elevate, and enrich that life, has been the province of those abundant spirits who poured their limitless thoughts and emotions into its limited forms. But it is precisely for the reason that a true artist is comprehensive that he may have something to say on the subject of morals, in which case our attention is attracted by the vigor of his thoughts and the beauty of his expression.

Moralists are generally determined to limit life. What they say is always in the nature of a prohibition. But this fact should not blind us to the truth that what is essentially a moral subject may be treated with exactly the opposite purpose in mind. Minister Smithy may hold up to his congregation the rewards of celibacy and the salvation inherent in prohibition, but also may Walt Whitman flatten out the Puritan dogma in its entirety and rear in its sickly stead a vigorous, electric growth. In

---

Toomer's review of Richard Aldington's "The Art of Poetry" (1921) is published here for the first time by permission of the Beinecke Rare Book and Manuscript Library, Yale University, New Haven, Connecticut.

so far as they deal with the rights and wrongs of human conduct, they are both moralists. For us the question is not "Did he treat of morals?" In the difference of their treatment lies the difference between the artist and the preacher.

Let us admit that most poetry cannot afford to be moralistic. But the reason for this we will have to seek in the poet rather than in the poetry. "The purpose of poetry is not ethical?" Certainly not. Any single purpose would limit it, and thus degrade it from an art form to that analogous to the pulpit.

Mr. Aldington says that "the old cant of a poet's 'message' is now completely discredited." These are certainly remarkable times we are living in. Transformations occur that leave the nature which produced a fish eye from nothing aghast. We of the Western world, whose thoughts have been shaped and moulded by the poets from Plato (Goethe, Ibsen, etc.) to Whitman suddenly roll on our backs with our face towards China and the Chinese. Charmed by their pictorial, suggestive loveliness we no longer hear the mighty voices of the past. Or rather, we hear them, but as a tired man hears a symphony; there is an auditory titillation, but no soul expansion—the spirit is too weary to respond.

I have used "we." I think it would be nearer the truth to say "they." By "they" meaning [Aldington] and similar ones whose eyes are so charmed and fascinated by the gem, by its outward appearance, by its external form, that the spirit behind the gem is not perceived. An exquisite image is preferred to a rousing message. Which is perfectly all right. I simply say that I do not believe such an attitude characteristic either of the Western poets or of their readers. Overnight our voice and our hearing have not shrunk into an eye. The deduction is that "messages" are now as always measured by their merit; that a fine message beautifully expressed, or a strong message vigorously expressed, will be accepted and appreciated now as much as in any former time.

After having relegated "message" poetry to the past, with seeming joy, in the very next paragraph Mr. Aldington seems to regret the fact that "literature seems out of touch with men's lives, with their real interests." That "we are very far from the times when a pamphlet by Chateaubriand re-established at least temporarily the dynasty of the Bourbons." Precisely so. And it is strange to me that Mr. Aldington overlooks the obvious logic of his point.

From Mr. Aldington's point of view, I think we can agree with him "that poetry is neither a means of ethical instruction, an after-dinner amusement, nor the lawful prey of souls and dilettantes."

II

Richard Aldington seeks personality. Where he finds that personality expressed in words, he is certain that he has found poetry. Whether prose or verse, or a mixture of them both is made use of, is merely a matter of distinction. "May we not then say that all good creative writing is poetry though this poetry has many forms?" I dare say. But we only slip one noose to get caught in another. What is and what isn't creative writing? To my mind one of those brilliant sallies of Bernard Shaw is certainly creative. And yet would we call it poetry? There is quite a difference between Shaw's *Man and Superman* and Shelley's *Julian and Madalo.* Both are instinct with personality. They are equally sincere, and in each the style is original and distinct. There is a difference. Nor may that difference be wholly explained with reference to their objective or subjective content. One is intellectual, the other emotional—essentially. At any rate they differ. And Mr. Aldington's "creative writing" does not explain it away.

Negro Psychology in The Emperor Jones

The Emperor Jones has already been explained, criticized, and accepted as an achievement in experimental dramatic form. Likewise, its significances for the Negro have been recognized. There remains, however, one aspect of the play which I find to be of unusual psychological interest, namely, the means employed by Mr. [Eugene] O'Neill to particularize the general emotion of fear in the Negro. It is obvious of course that a distinct racial flavor is created by having a Negro act the part of Brutus Jones. But this has to do with presentation, and not with the actual construction of the drama. In this construction, Mr. O'Neill first establishes fear by means of suggestion and association. This original feeling is increased by physical circumstances: a forest, and the beating of a tom-tom. And then, as fear intensifies to the point where it overpowers Jones, it successively unlocks chambers of the Emperor's unconscious. Now the contents of the unconscious not only vary with individuals; they are differentiated because of race, by social conditions due to race. And in fact Brutus Jones lives through sections of an unconscious which is peculiar to the Negro. Slave ships, whipping posts, and so on. And because these things are actually real and present for him, his fear is at once expressed, intensified, and colored by them. In a word, his fear becomes a Negro's fear, recognizably different from a similar emotion, modified by other racial experience. In this way then, Mr. O'Neill achieves his purpose. And *The Emperor Jones* is therefore a section of Negro psychology presented in significant dramatic form.

"Negro Psychology in The Emperor Jones" (1921) is published here by permission of the Beinecke Rare Book and Manuscript Library, Yale University, New Haven, Connecticut.

Waldo Frank's Holiday

Though Southern materials make up the body of this novel, the primary approach to it should not be sectional. Rather, one should come to it through the artistic personality of Waldo Frank. This attitude is natural to those who have experienced the author's *Rahab* and *City Block.* For these works frankly eschew geographical and naturalistic fidelity in favour of a reality more individual and more essentialized. In like manner, *Holiday* is first of all a subjective design; it has utilized certain elements of the South because these seemed most suited to its purposes. Hence whatever local or racial truth or untruth the work may contain must be considered as a purely secondary factor.

The design is stark and clear enough. It is concerned with repression and release, with repression and expression, as consequent and contrasting realities of human life. But the design, as achieved in novelistic form, is dynamic. Therefore it manipulates the effects and frictions of these realities to create its movement and its climaxes.

Frank is too subtle for an arbitrary portioning of repression, in a block, to the whites of the South; for a rigid symbolizing of the blacks as expression. He sees the Negro as free within a very strict oppression. He sees the white—half, respectably restricted, half, frankly-hypocritically loose—compressed by an equally strict freedom. Each race then, within itself, contains the contrasting elements. And he knows that the Negro often serves as outlet for the pent energies of the dominant race. In contrast with each other, however, it may be said that in this novel the blacks generally represent a full life; while the whites stand for a denial

"Waldo Frank's *Holiday*" originally appeared in *Dial* 75 (Oct. 1923): 383–86.

of it. The black church, the white church; niggertown, whitetown, are similarly opposed. This opposition gets its statement in the opening passage: "Sunset at Nazareth. Niggers go home through the copper-glow of pines. Niggers sing home. White men stand lean in the doors of paintless houses. White men stand still." And by means of swift chapter juxtapositions, and the Frankian crystallizations of unspoken consciousness, it is sustained throughout the book.

For the purpose of a novel, and likewise in order that Frank's intentions be completely realized, it was necessary that two bodies, a white and a black, be set in movement, through the contrasting states, towards each other. Virginia Hade and John Cloud, vehicles for a need conscious beyond the local taboos placed upon sex and race, move towards each other. Away from Nazareth, where nature is still innocent of the divisions that spring to life with exploitation, they meet. For the first moments their contact is as clean as nature is. And then the inevitable differences and discords assert themselves. Having exchanged knives with her, the black man suddenly recalls, "I am John Cloud. Nigger." Whereupon he straightway leaves her. She, pressing his knife into her waist, cuts herself. The wound is a mere body-outlet. Deeper release has been denied. Conscious that her own world is the real cause of her frustration, she nevertheless fastens upon John as the immediate instrument of it. And, impelled by a force, clearly greater than volition, with John's knife still in her hand, and blood upon her, she marches into the town square. White Nazareth is just coming from a revival which has whipped it to within an inch of release. Full release, not quite. It sees Virginia, Cloud's knife, and it immediately knows that a lynching will fulfill what the revival failed in. "—Upon the black branch of the black tree let there be Fruit! Let there be seed, let there be fruit for my passion!" It forthwith gets John Cloud and hangs him. "Nazareth beneath him peers with grimed eyes through the murk of its spent lust." Virginia, comfortable in bed, makes no effort to avert the tragedy she senses taking place: "—Who made this wound? My hand. Yet it is your wound, John." Here, then, [are] the design and motorplot of *Holiday.*

They are executed with a precision, an economy, a swiftness, and a sense of form that spell artistic mastery. Generally, the aesthetic employed is that so accurately analyzed by Gorham B. Munson in his *Waldo Frank: A Study.* The Frankian aesthetic of mobility ". . . accomplished first of all by the abundant use of very active verbs . . . generated by his shrewd calculation of overstatements, by his thrusting and expanding figures of speech . . . worked up by lyrical crystallizations, by swift dramatic presentation, by the alternating structure of the Whole"—adapted to the given materials. In this review I shall concentrate upon Frank's use of the unspoken consciousness, for in *Holiday,* more than in any previous work, this is a major element of his aesthetic.

Considered as a structural mechanism, it provides the condensation, swiftness, and dramatic contrasts essential to such a design as *Holiday.* The psychology of a repressed people, seeking release in a revival tent, is given in seven lines, the last of which reads "Come, preacher, lash us! Make us leap!" Virginia Hade's consciousness is unfolded in seven lyric pages. And whitetown and niggertown, taken as entities, are vividly opposed in the same number. I quote from this section:

> "How can I rest in you when you stand and shout? I am weary with whiteness. To rule, to be civilized and chaste; you do not know what weariness it is. My woman yearns towards me in hunger I am spent. All the world waves in darkling circles about my white uprightness, I am spent. Your pools draw my blood: your red soils blanch me dry. I must lie in you! But you who are my earth stand up and shout! How can I rest in you? How can I shut my eyes?
> —Leave me alone
> Don' you see we is lovin'?
> Leave me alone . . .
> Don' tell me nothin',
> How kin I listen to you
> When mah love's lips
> When mah love's arms
> When de soft breast ob mah love
> Closes roun' me like de earth
> . . . all laughin flowers
> Comes roun' me like de air
> . . . all smilin' breeze."

As functions of the larger organism, these crystallizations are effective and admirable.

Considered in relation to specific characters, they operate fanwise. By their means, the figures expand to an awareness which otherwise would be impossible to them. Because this extra-awareness raises the conscious level of the book, because it contributes to Frank's general intention, it is justified. It nevertheless forces one to accept the characters as essentially Frankian in origin. There is no valid artistic reason why an author should not project portions of himself into his characters. In fact there is a very definite artistic reason why he should. For this is the method of great creation. But he should be fully determined in this position. And no trace of an incongruent mode should be allowed to infringe it. The figures, of whatever origin, should stand consonant and fused. In *Holiday*, here and there are to be found breaks in texture, of the dialogue, of the dialogue compared to the unspoken consciousness, that make one question Frank's clarity, during the process of composition, on this point. For example, take these lines attributed to John Cloud:

> "Ol' woman—yo' getting lazy, yo' gettin' fat! Yo' cookin's too good.
> Mammy, soon I'll have to h'ist you."
> "—*It is your skin!*
>   —Your love's a white sun shinin' on a sea.
>   Summer blue sea
>   Summer blue sky
>   . . . Da's your love!
> *It is your skin!*"
> "—I love you, mother. But it is your fault. You made me."
> "—An' I care fo' you. An' in my love fo' you, why is there blame?"

I do not of course refer to any superficial difference in the language used, in the use of dialect. I refer to a psychological break, a too obvious duality of origin which suspends one between the desire to accept Cloud as a Southern Negro, and the desire to accept him as a character created by Frank for the specific purposes of his design. This break is the one serious interior defect that I find in *Holiday*. It does not, however, impair the structural finish of this novel. Technically, it is solid and tight. And as an art form it is clean, superb. *Holiday* therefore sustains Waldo Frank's high achievement as a literary artist.

The South in Literature

Within the last decade, American letters have been vitalized by the maturation of a sectional art. New England, through the personalities of Robert Frost and Edward Arlington Robinson, and the Middle West, articulated in Sherwood Anderson, Theodore Dreiser, Carl Sandburg, and Edgar Lee Masters, have each contributed notably to the general leavening. This fact already belongs to the literary history of America. It is natural therefore that cultured minds should turn expectantly towards the South. That they should feel certain that here too a splendid birth was imminent. For surely no other section is so rich in the crude materials and experiences prerequisite to art. The South has a peasantry, rooted in its soil, such as neither the North nor West possesses. Therefore, it has a basic adjustment to its physical environment (in sharp contrast to the restless maladjustment of the Northern pioneer) the expression of which the general cultural body stands in sore need of. And rising from its agricultural communities there spreads a Southern life of rich complexity. Factories, main streets, and survivals of the old plantations roughly chart these degrees. It has the stark theme of white and black races. But above all, the South is a land of the great passions: hate, fear, cruelty, courage, love, and aspiration. And it possesses a tradition of leisure by means of

---

According to Darwin Turner, and later Therman B. O'Daniel (who duplicates what is ostensibly an error), "The South in Literature" was published in *The Call* in 1923. Despite extensive research, I have been unable to locate this essay in *The Call*, and have therefore used the Beinecke Library copy. It is published here by permission of the Beinecke Rare Book and Manuscript Library, Yale University, New Haven, Connecticut.

which these attributes might find their way into a significant culture. Nor has the South ever lacked a moderate share of the nation's literary talent. Why then, one inevitably asks, has it not contributed an equivalent achievement to our sectional art? It is the purpose of this paper to present two books: *Holiday,* by Waldo Frank, and *Cane,* by Jean Toomer, a brief survey of which will convince the reader that, through [these novels] the South is an important, though it may not yet be an equivalent contributor to the general ferment now evident in American letters.

Since the juxtaposition of the white and black races is so typical of Southern life, it is of real interest to know that the authors of these books are personally expressive of this racial contrast. For Waldo Frank is of white, while Jean Toomer is of Negro descent. In the past, these bloods have too often used their heritage and Southern materials as reasons for and means of social propaganda. But Frank and Toomer are not thus concerned with a limiting of life to rival claims. These men are artists. Life in its totality is sweet to them. And their mission is to stamp its essences with the forms of art. Inevitably, of course, racial difference has its function in pure literature. It is, for instance, quite frequently the basis for those temperamental variations which so delight the experienced reader. In this way, the white and black races are contrasted and utilized in Waldo Frank and Jean Toomer, in *Holiday* and *Cane.*

* * *

Holiday is a novel whose scene is laid in a small present day gulf [coast] town. Nazareth is typically Southern, for it is divided into white[town] and niggertown. Her red soil blazes beneath a white hot sky. Pine and cypress swamps, canebrakes and cottonfields flank it.

Whitetown, with its main street, electric lamps, drugstores, movies, and specialty shops, is similar in its commercial unloveliness to thousands of villages, North and South and West, that dot the country. It leans away from its agricultural past. It strains towards the larger cities, towards the mode of life definitely stamped by American industrialism. And its people are the products of this straining. . . . In truth, white Nazareth might well be a second Gopher Prairie but for the fact that a black Nazareth, juxtaposed to it, insistently determines mind-habits and emotional states that are peculiar to the South.

The cabins and the black peasantry of niggertown are ingrown products of the soil. Negroes are as firmly rooted as the pine trees are. Like these trees, black men sprout to life with movement circumscribed. And, as in the case with all healthy natural life, desire, and desire's satisfaction, are inseparable elements of their growth. Hence, in niggertown there is no urge to found the restlessness towards industrial complexity. Negroes work with their hands in soil. They cook, they eat, sing, love, and go to sleep. But Negroes know the tangency of whitetown. When they think about it, they are oppressed. When they feel it, they fear or hate. And sometimes whitetown becomes a dream which arises from no one of these states. A dream whose web is woven of those poignant longings, too impalpable to be satisfied by immediate life, too concrete to be deferred to possible fulfillment in a distant Camp Ground. Affected by the dark uncertain movements of niggertown, whitetown reacts in ways typically Southern. The plot of *Holiday* is concerned with these acts and reactions.

Virginia Hade, daughter of the wealthiest white man in town, is compressed and restricted by the conventional limitations of white Nazareth. But the restlessness, thus engendered, does not seek an easy surface release in the complications of a larger city. Rather, because of it, Virginia becomes introspective. She comes to know herself and her own needs. And she sees local taboos as so many artificial barriers erected against the natural expressions of them. Thus clear as to her own demands, she still is somewhat vague about the objects to be utilized, she still is somewhat passive concerning the methods to be initiated for her purposes. In this state of suspension and uncertainty she walks to work one morning, to the offices of her father's company.

Meanwhile, John Cloud, Negro, sensitive to the rich taste and color of black Southern life, sensitive too to the oppression and hatred, derivatives of whitetown, and to the dream which it evokes, has left niggertown for the day's work in Hade's business. White men upon the streets resent his easeful dignity as he passes them. They taunt and finally insult him. Cloud moves on. He walks up the street behind Virginia. Judge Hade also goes to his offices. He sees Virginia, John Cloud, and the curious dream-look in the latter's eyes. At work, he finds his daughter dreaming. The day is too hot to work, so at Cloud's suggestion Virginia declares a holiday. The Negro hands go off. White Nazareth fills a revival tent. The preacher uses Biblical words to lash them. But the lashing does not bring relief. John and Virginia meet in a wooded spot just outside the town limits. For one pure moment their meeting fulfills the dream in each. But sustained and complete contact is to be denied them. For Cloud, recalling the fact that he is a Negro, after having exchanged knives with her, abruptly leaves. Whereupon Virginia cuts herself with Cloud's knife and walks back to the village square. White Nazareth, just [back] from the revival tent, sees her. The tell-tale knife. A mob of lynchers forms. They snake into niggertown, get the black man, return with him, and while the congregation, only a few moments removed from Christ, looks on, hang him. Virginia, whose word would stay the rope, is held by a blind power away from the scene. Anyone at all familiar with the South will recognize this scene and plot and these materials as typical of it. Waldo Frank's literary genius has fleshed them in this novel with a rare beauty and a deep rich sense of life.

Cane is a collection of poems, short stories, and one long drama, all of which are notable for their lyricism and evocation of the Southern atmosphere. There are three sub-divisions of this book.

The materials of Part One are those of middle Georgia. Poem and short story themes arise from a symphony of red soil, pine trees, cane-brakes and cotton fields, swamps, saw-mills, old Negro cabins, and hills and valleys saturate with the blood and toil, the songs and sufferings of the slave regime. The themes themselves weave about young Negro girls whose dusky loveliness flowers for a moment, yields to the insistent claims of love, then fades, as all natural beauty must, to the inconspicuous monotone of surrounding landscape. One story tells of a white woman who had two Negro sons. Of how the conventions ruled her out of social friendship, and all the while the human instincts in both white and black folk fed her and cared for her more tenderly than if she had been permitted to continue living in the town. Another sketch relates the futile love of an emotionally thin woman for a truly epic Negro. And the last story of this section is built around the love of a black and a white man for the same girl. The story ends in a lynching. Readers of these two books will find it of interest to compare the temperamental approach to this theme with the approach to the similar one in *Holiday.*

In Part Two the milieu shifts to Washington, but it is still Southern and still Negro. Here, however, the slow peasant rhythm, the peasants basic adjustment to his physical environment give way to more strident cadences. And the life becomes more conscious, more restless and stirring, and hence more complex. But the soft loveliness of the city streets, the rich warm taste of dark-skinned life, and the music and the humor give a pervasive sub-tone which is distinctly of the South. This [is] a section of spiritual growth and psychological subtlety. And the frustrations of love and aspiration yield a power considerably greater than that of [Part One]. The outline of one story must here suffice. A deeply sensitive young man offers his love to a woman who is prevented by conventional restrictions from accepting it. Later, while witnessing a vaudeville show, these very conventions (embodied in the audience) demand that she accept the coarser passion which an actor from the stage in mock-play tries to force on her. Much against her will, she does. The irony and unfairness of this episode whip the young fellow to a frenzy. There in the theatre he rises to his feet and gains release by shouting. The design of this story is to dramatically present the ironic contrasts of a love directed by convention.

Part Three, a single drama, swings back to middle Georgia. Here again one finds the hills and valleys resonant with folk songs, saturate with the pain and joy, the ugliness and beauty of a peasant people. The elemental pulse of these, together with the impalpable fog of white dominance and its implications which the raw sensibility of Ralph Kabnis (the protagonist) spreads over the entire countryside, are too strong and oppressive for his depleted energies to successfully grapple with. Hence Kabnis progresses downward from rejection and defiance to a passive acceptance of them. Such acquiescence, in a man potentially capable of directing life, signifies frustration and defeat. This drama then is the tragedy of a talented Negro whose forces have been dissipated, whose remaining strength is unequal to the task of winning a clear way through life. Its properties are graphic and compelling: soliloquies wherein weakness and power, fear, courage, curses and adoration swiftly alternate; solid and vividly defined minor characters; their dialog, its tang, soil-ness, and lyricism; scenes—Negro cabins, a wagon shop, a cellar of debauchery and prayer—whose life and movement spring from the stark impact of opposing wills and naked passions. But a detailed account of these properly belongs to dramatic analysis. One may quote here, however, a critical statement by Gorham B. Munson, the author of *Waldo Frank: A Study* and editor of the left-wing literary organ, *Secession*: "'Kabnis' is an American equivalent to a Russian drama by Maxim Gorki or Anton [Chekhov]. It ramifies deeply into the soil and into life, and it reaches up to a stunted broken intellectualism. But it is not simply a thick concentration of Southern Negro life. Cadenced speech, off-stage song, fantastic settings, character development and character interplay mingle to create a design of sufficient power to carry its important significances. Its production should be undertaken by an American equivalent to the Moscow Art Theatre, which unhappily does yet not exist."

Cane, then, is so evidently Southern in content. As to its literary execution, I give the concluding passage of Waldo Frank's Foreword to this book: "The notes of [Toomer's] counterpoint are particular, the themes are of intimate connection with us Americans. But the result is that abstract and absolute thing called Art."

* * *

The foregoing survey, sketchy of necessity, is sufficient to establish the claims with which this paper started. For in these books, *Holiday* and *Cane,* one finds the South: its peasantry, its complex life above the agricultural communities, the stark theme of the white and black races, and the sweep of its great passions. And finally, because of their sheer literary achievement, one finds here the South as a significant contributor to our [American] sectional art.

Review of Zona Gale's Faint Perfume

A mild and somewhat passive sensitivity in contact with life's innocuous commonplaces yields two primary states: a poignance, and an awareness proportioned to the degree of sensitivity. *Faint Perfume,* the story of a delicate woman shunted temporarily into the family of a Gideonite, receiving her love experience in the midst, is less successful in realizing the first than the second of these. The book is emotionally thin, and curiously without body. Hence the impacts, frictions, and distress that it should generate never really move one. Though the boy, Oliver, responding in the spontaneous manner of childhood to life's quick shifts from joy to pain, is satisfying in this respect. But the positive feature of this novel is the delicate awareness that illumines its pages. Particularly, the awareness that springs into being with the love episode. It is a fine thing in these days to be reminded and convinced that the contact of a man and a woman can result in something beyond sex[ual] conflict; in an expansion, in an intensification of life generally. And it is pleasant in current fiction to read such statements of inner and outer relationship as these:

> "Leda was shaken by an abrupt sense that they were one creature, as if each had extensions of being which had fused in something finer than light and color, had become one consciousness." "At this she laughed, thinking how in his presence one became multiplied, arrived at more being. But she was afraid to tell him so. Not afraid of him essentially,

---

Toomer's review of Zona Gale's *Faint Perfume* (1923) originally appeared in *Broom* 5 (Oct. 1923): 180–81.

> but rather of his external and worldly self, the guest of that house." "How is anyone to survive talk which leaves one physically faint from its unconscious breaches of decency?" "It was an intense affirmation to sit there saying nothing."

In fact, the fault and fineness of the book lie in just this: that it gives the reality of perception rather than that of dimensional experience; that its movement is achieved by no motors below the level of sensitized perception. If the following quotation be taken as the central idea of *Faint Perfume*: "There awaited her that new horror, new by only a few thousand years, which attends on the emergence of sensibility: The new horror of an isolated sensibility wared upon by the still insensible flesh of the race from which it rises" then it may be concluded that while this sensibility is given, the horror, the emotion, is not realized.

Open Letter to Gorham Munson

I liked your piece in *S4N*: the concentration on America, the acceptance of the machine, the attitude (the only healthy, the only *art* attitude) which uses modern forms, and not the hurt caused by them, as the basis of a national literature. (The life around me is pregnant and warm, dynamic, tensioned, massed, jazzed, lovable. If my dinner digests well, I love it. There is no spiritual resistance. I had been in every powerhouse in the city years before I dragged myself into the Corcoran Gallery. And I neglected the 'poetry of the people' for such things as motorcycle motors, dynamos and generators. The first thing that I made from cardboard was a battleship. There is not a statue in Washington with the living beauty of line and balance of certain Pierce-Arrow cars. And the National Museum looks mouldy beside any automobile show window.)

But there is something lacking in your program. Take the machine: you get form, simplification, at least the basis for strangeness, abstraction. All right. Does that exhaust your machine? Not by a damned sight. A toy model of a machine would give you these. What's lacking in the toy? Power, friend, power! And if *Secession* doesn't watch itself, there's where it is going to fall down. Not in criticism, but in imaginative writing. Your imaginative writing too easily thins out into what is trivial and inconsequential and weak. A weak machine is ready for the scrap heap. Whatever its design, what significance is there to a machine rusting in a junkman's yard? What to a poem, sketch or novel that lacks stuff, power, deep organic functioning? That can do no work?

"Open Letter to Gorham Munson" originally appeared in *S4N* 25 (Mar. 1923).

To me, these considerations do not raise the weary question as to whether or not the purely aesthetic in literature is the prime factor, is exhaustive, is sufficient. This thought does come to me: that the dualism of form and substance is largely specious, that great design does not rise from puny matter. The form of a machine for dislocating fly joints would inspire no one. The form of a sketch that locates fly joints can claim no greater virtue. I want great art. This means I want great design. As a means to this end, I want great substance, great power.

Notations on The Captain's Doll

The purpose of the three stories, *The Captain's Doll, The Fox,* and *The Ladybird,* grouped in this volume is to convey a serious sense of the unusual. For this enterprise, Mr. D. H. Lawrence employs the following equipment:

(1) a narrative technique which makes use of symbols: a doll, a fox, a ladybird, to gear and regulate the tales. Necessarily, the results are rather slight and somewhat artificial, for such devices can be nothing more than anemic substitutes for the natural depth and drive of generative ideas and essentialized design.

In the first story, a portrait doll of Captain Hepburn, made by his mistress, is dangled about until it is forced to serve as starting point for the following observation: "And you can say what you like, but *any* woman, today, no matter *how* much she loves her man—she could start any minute and make a doll of him. And the doll would be her hero: and her hero would be no more than her doll."

Which is the climax of this episode. The fox is more effectively an instrument of the second narrative. For the effect it has upon the girl Ellen, and the compelling fascination which Henry Grenfel exercises over her are similar and interchangeable. But the importance and function of the ladybird, aside from certain irrelevant comments made concerning it and the fact that it is a descendant of the Egyptian scarabaeus, are questionable, trivial.

"Notations on *The Captain's Doll*" originally appeared in *Broom* 5 (Aug. 1923): 47–49.

(2) A descriptive faculty that tends to overshadow or ignore the essential progression of the characters. Excessive and repeated description of a glacier, for example, all but obliterates the central figures who technically should be working towards a rapid climax while ascending it. This over-description often comes in large undigested chunks directly to the reader. Hence the characters are not served by it. Rather, one feels that they exist for the purposes of the description. This faculty is perhaps at its best when concerned with physical attractiveness. "The women, old and young, paraded in the peasant-costume, in flowery cotton dresses with gaudy, expensive silk aprons: the men wore the Tyrolese costume, bare knees and little short jackets. And for the men the correct thing was to have the leathern hose and the blue linen jacket as old as possible. If you had a hole in your leathern seat, so much the better."

(3) An ability to conceive, but not to inevitably unfold and realize character. Doubtless the five or six major figures of this volume were possessed with unusual qualities and important problems of development, as Mr. Lawrence saw them. And it must be granted that as creations Captain Hepburn, Ellen March, Grenfel, and Psanek have a certain objective validity. The soft, amusing indifference and indecision of the first, Ellen's rapid shifts from surface efficiency to deep, subconscious dreams and brooding, Grenfel's foxiness and determination, Psanek's solitary hate and his intense sub-surface power—these qualities exist in the pages of this book. But because Mr. Lawrence fails to finally grip and develop them, they tend to a static rather than to a dynamic and cumulative reality. Hence one sees them; one does not always feel and know them to be there. And with his minor figures Mr. Lawrence is even less successful. Why Hepburn's mistress, for example, should invariably be amazed at him is anything but clear. To state that she is, by the repeated use of this convention: "in the midst of her indignant amazement" or "she turned on him with wide-open eyes of amazement" simply begs the labor of convincing creation. And so, the relations between Hepburn and his lover approach the absurd. In fact the element of absurdity is often so near the surface of these tales, that one with difficulty restrains the conviction that Mr. Lawrence is laughing all the while.

(4) A prose style, not far removed from the accents and texture of conversation, most at ease in dialog, most competent in narrative passages and in description. A style rarely or never luminous and dense, muscular and racy. Nor has it those finished periods that distinguish traditional English prose. Cliche, ineffective images and figures of speech, however, generously stud it:

"It was all like a mystery to her, as if one of the men from Mars were loving her"; "it was exactly like day in some other planet"; "he was just committed to her, as he might have been committed to gaol, or committed to paradise"; "so he had seemed to her: like a mute Caesar. Like Germanicus"; "the strange look, like destiny, in his wide-open, almost staring eyes"; "she could feel the arrows of desire rankling"; "but also, the queer figure that sat alone on the roof watching the stars!" "The wonderful red flower of the cactus"; "like a flown bird"; "and you giving off beams of bright effulgence like a Gloria!" "it (the glacier) seemed to her like a grand beast"; "so, after a while of this valley of the shadow of death."

And so on. Now one or two more acceptable images by way of balance:

"The sky from above was like a sharp wedge forcing its way into the earth's cleavage, and that eternal ferocious water was like the steel edge of the wedge, the terrible tip biting into the rock's intensity;" "she could faintly see the flesh through his beard, as water through reeds." "'Yes, I do know what you are talking about. Yes, I do,' he persisted softly, as if he were producing his voice in her blood."

(5) A solemnity of background and underlying temperament, an evidently earnest purpose that destroys the fun one might have from those incidents that are frankly absurd, or approach the absurd. Take the passage where Hepburn is frightened at seeing himself in a still-life painting along with two sunflowers in a glass and a poached egg on toast. Quite amusing, really. But immediately following this we are assured that the Captain is not a person to be spoofed with, for "fatigued and furious he arrived in Salzburg, seeing no beauty in anything." And the whole thing is spoiled.

This seriousness will not permit of the volume being taken as a bit of incidental writing. Unfortunately, on no other basis can one claim for it a literary value.

The Critic of Waldo Frank: Criticism, An Art Form

Gorham B. Munson's expressional activity, when writing his *Waldo Frank: A Study,* was a compound of three elements: esthetic analysis, cultural criticism, and the shaping of a dynamic form. These elements, penetrating, accurate, enthusiastic, controlled, were manipulating unusually adequate material: the novels of Waldo Frank, *Our America,* and Frank's literary career. The *Study* then, on three counts, is an achievement. It is the first contemporary American esthetic analysis of the novel. It is the first work to contain an opposing, a consequent vision at all commensurate with that of *Our America.* And, for the reason that it attains to structural significance, it is an art product in the critical form.

1

Munson's approach to the successive novels *The Unwelcome Man* and *The Dark Mother, Rahab* and *City Block,* is varied; but his method invariably deposits, clearly, accurately, these elements of each novel: substance; esthetic; temperamental content, that is, its relation to Waldo Frank as author; and its relation to the work which precedes or follows it. And as is necessary, his method includes comment and judgment.

The substance of *The Unwelcome Man* is deeply significant. As background, a small town in Long Island, college, and New York City. Quincy Burt's family fits soddenly into the first and last of these. Burt himself, spiritually gifted, maladjusted, frets against his environment, and is finally

"The Critic of Waldo Frank: Criticism, An Art Form" originally appeared in *S4N* 30 (Jan. 1924).

absorbed by the Stream. Psychology and social criticism of a first-rate order are woven into this structure. But the book is judged an organic failure because Quincy "should be and is not the central energy." Being a first book, of such material, esthetic success is not expected of it. Its diction however is concise, and here and there are found the beginnings of a unique style.

In the matter of relationship I find Munson's analysis incomplete. *The Unwelcome Man* contains a vivid contrast of Nature and the City. Or, if you will, of Nature and the consequences of Industrialism. Quincy, spiritually mutilated by the latter, seeks an understanding of his pain, a healing, at least a momentary surcease of conflict, in weeds and trees and flowers. Futilely. For Nature is a mute mother, herself challenged by encroaching Forms. She is powerless to help him. Hence Burt, with no technic by means of which he can meet the extensions of the Machine, is completely wilted. Well then, the logic of this book demands that such a technic be found. Frank is forced to fashion it. And *Our America*, in its aspect of anti-body, is the direct result. It is this relationship, or this significance, which Munson does not establish.

The Dark Mother is a widening, a deepening, above all a *penetrating* of certain basic materials contained in *The Unwelcome Man.* Here the milieu is denser. And in this novel it can almost be said that Nature and the small town are completely overshadowed by the City. New York, its complicated social texture, its buildings, its movement, its dirt and filth and its crude beauty, aggregate a dimensioned life which makes the efforts of other novelists and poets seem tentative and puny. Into this heaving mass comes David. His is a slow-moving organic life, rooted within its own spiritual unfolding, and for this reason, sufficient. The complex, rational, cynical Tom cannot budge him. Nor can Cornelia. After his own fashion David survives the City.

This novel too is judged an esthetic failure, albeit it is an exciting one. Its merits are clear:

> The diction, it is true, has an occasional touch of rhetoric, but in the main it shows a smooth short rhythm, directness when needed, an exact freshness in figures of speech, and a vers libre derivation that makes it more individual than that of *The Unwelcome Man.* The rocking flux of the opening paragraphs is a contribution to the technic of introductions. And the climax, David's entrance into Cornelia's Thanksgiving Day tea, is superbly planned and brought off. . . the component parts of this book are sometimes subtle, sometimes profound, often moving. The author has constructed his characters in his mind, he has an environment to impinge on them, he has a vital drama for them to play.

Why then, the failure? In answering this question, Munson, using the psychological approach of Paul Rosenfeld as contrasting material, has an excellent opportunity to apply the esthetic solution. I give his conclusion:

> The trouble with *The Dark Mother* is purely esthetic: it lies solely in its technic and its form. The form of *The Dark Mother* is standard enough: it is Flaubertian with its single plane and exterior treatment of consciousness. It obliged Frank to discuss his characters, and it is true, as Mr. Rosenfeld objected, he "discusses, discusses, discusses his characters". The significant thing is that with Frank these discussions swathe his characters in writing; they are inert and lifeless. They leave little creation for the reader to do. Waldo Frank's instrument, psychoanalysis, has been too devastating. Its over-use has killed the energies of his counters. Assuredly, character-discussions as a method are alien to him. Still more significant is the sense of rubbing against the formal mould, the strain manifest here and there in *The Dark Mother.* It is for that we may call *The Dark Mother* a transitional novel, for this strain may portend the birth of a new form. What is clear, at least, is that it indicates a discord between the temperament of Waldo Frank and the esthetic adopted, a war between him and the method.

In as much as this temperament is robust and abundant, one naturally asks, Will its true esthetic be found? *Rahab* is the answer to this question.

Rahab is the climax of the work of Waldo Frank. And the analysis of *Rahab* is the climax of this *Study.* It is superb. One knows from it that the novel as an art form in America has its critic. Further, taking it as a sufficient unit, the manipulation of its structure reveals Munson as an artist in the critical form. I should like to quote it in the whole. *Rahab*'s passionate, transforming religious content; its esthetic of lyric, dramatic mobility: active verbs, expanding images, lyric crystallizations, swift dramatic shifts, fluxes terminating in decisive statements; its form in relation to the moving picture; its triumphant use of the throw-back; and so on. Here Munson achieves a brilliant condensation. The body of the story takes form, and the story's significant curve emerges. *Rahab*'s technical achievements; punctuation, rests, mood-poems; and so on. "It is one of our few contemporary satisfaction[s]." And I say Yea! to that, and to his own analysis. I do think, though, that in point of presentation he stopped just one step short. Munson is aware of lyric crystallizations as specific elements in Frank's larger structure. But, despite his statements as regards its esthetic of mobility, he does not make it clear that this larger structure itself is nothing less than a lyric crystallization of which the interior poems and images are the facets. This, I think to be true. And I consider emphasis of this fact important because it gives at a glance the logic of Frank's organization.

City Block, as an esthetic form, is too close, it contains too much speculative matter to allow of Munson's analyzing it in the definitive way that *Rahab* is handled. Is it a spherical form, do the stories fit into an inevitable circle, is there a curve cementing them together and giving the Whole a dynamic propulsion forward? Munson thinks there is, and I am of his opinion. But we are still too close to really know. Certain things, however, are definite: the perfection of its component units (one of which Munson splendidly analyses); the unity of subject matter; further technical achievements; the terrific impact of *City Block* in terms of dimensioned experience. This book, in short, carries every potential of greatness. It but awaits complete realization within our own slow-moving minds. Munson observes that "Beginning" in *City Block* rounds this volume off "in an outer circle of quiet." And I might add, there is a quality in *City Block,* for all its spiritual drama and intensity, that encloses Frank's work to date in a rare white pulsing stillness.

What next? Munson feels that towards the end, *City Block* has a tendency to dissolve, that like *The Dark Mother* it gives evidences of transition, and that, again like *The Dark Mother,* it may presage a new esthetic. Perhaps. At any rate, Waldo Frank's achievements now challenge a contemporary placement. As regards literary movements, his mystical realism, his esthetic concern, swing him far beyond the limits of the naturalists and surface realists in this country. It follows that his is a lonely eminence. In terms of world literature, Munson confines himself to a swift contrast of Frank with James Joyce. Without here going into details, I think it accurate to conclude that there is a wide difference between these men. . . . Frank sweeps on. There are no signs of dryness or of slackening in his genius.

2

The *Study,* as cultural criticism, may readily be grouped under three headings: (1) Interpretation of *Our America,* (2) The positing of an opposing, or, better, a consequent vision, (3) A valuing of *Our America* in the light of (2).

I think Munson would have done well to have included in this phase a fourth function, namely, that of relating *Our America* to *The Unwelcome Man.* In the first section of this review I stated that *Our America,* in its aspect of anti-body, seems to have been the direct result of Frank's facing the conclusion of his first book. It is equally true that *Our America,* as a passionate singing form, is a sweep away from the dead levels of *The Unwelcome Man.* To have sharply contrasted the two, with this fact in mind, would have established a deep emotional logic. This logic, while not necessary to esthetic analysis, is vital, I feel, to a knowledge and grasp of Waldo Frank as the "central energy" of this *Study.*

Munson does however bring a fine intelligence and enthusiasm to bear upon this book. In a single passage he gives a condensation and a judgment that will stand:

> Swift, rhythmical, dynamic; passionate, optimistic and singing; economical, imagistic, energetic; intelligent, documented and, above all, controlled. Its diverse materials absorb into a forward-moving logic which rises into thrilling prophecy at the end. The book points. It functions freely. It synthesizes the researches of Randolph Bourne and Van Wyck Brooks, develops them, and gives them an irresistible drive. It is an achievement.

Our America contains a concept of these States. This concept is saturate with religion. Walt Whitman would recognize it. This concept also embodies a criticism of psychoanalytical derivation which is leveled at the pioneer and puritan. To successfully controvert it, one would have to undermine the science it rests upon. In addition, *Our America* comes to grips with industrialism. In this latter phase Munson finds that it functions as an anti-body, that is, as an organ created for the purpose of minimizing the negative aspects, the positive ravages of the Machine. And it is here that our critic gives, in tentative opposition, his own cultural program.

Briefly stated, this program is as follows: There are now three factors in the spiritual life of man: man himself, Nature, and the Machine. The Machine, when first introduced, destroyed the balance which man had achieved with Nature, and the old art of adjustment gave way to a disjointed art. To date, the art of maladjustment has tried to meet man's spiritual conflicts in two ways: first, by a total rejection of the Machine, that is, by a back-to-nature program; second, by accepting the Machine as a necessary evil and erecting against it certain counter-forms. The former of these has been demonstrated to be impotent. The latter, despite the body of the first rate literature that it has produced, may in reality resolve into nothing more vital than a compromise, a dualism, "an antagonism superficially similar to that between man and nature promulgated by the puritans." If this be true, then it follows that man must override this dualism, that he must evolve a creative amalgam of himself, Nature, and the Machine. Dadaism in Europe, in addition to its attempted destruction of counter-forms, has for its purpose this specific purpose. But though it has achieved

> a species of mechanized art, one capable of carrying intellect, courage, humor, aggressiveness, tension, speed, of giving minor esthetic thrills, (up) till now, it has refused to channel emotional profundities, to take up love and desire and religion into its form. But while thus so patently limited, it should still be encouraged. For if my tentatives should prove to be sound, then we are in the childhood of a new age, we are, by the chronological accident of birth, chosen to create the simple forms, the folk-tales and folk-music the preliminary art that our descendants may utilize in the vast struggle to put positive and glowing spiritual content into Machinery.

There is logic and health, joy and contagion in this vision. It has a tremendous appeal to me personally. For as much as I respect the suffering caused by the Machine, as much as I respond to that suffering when esthetically presented, my own reaction to everything from penny engines to turbines, from Pierce-Arrows to battleships, is one continuous pleasure. But to relate this vision to that of *Our America.*

If this triangular culture in truth tallies with the future, then Munson concluded that *Our America* underestimates jazz, electric signs, motion-pictures, skyscrapers, etc., and that its future is a limited one. With the first of these assertions I agree. In fact I would say that even now its understatement of these modern factors is evident. As to the limited future, based upon the reasons given in this *Study,* I believe Munson to be wrong. It seems to me that his insight has been crippled in two ways. First, he holds *Our America,* the anti-body, too close to his eye, though perhaps no one better knows its positive elements. Second, a phase of Munson's program gets it vitality and stimulus from hard-fisted rejection. In this case, he has sacrificed a probable, a comparatively distant truth to an immediate need. For it is clear, surely, that once the triangular culture is well under way, it can then be tolerant of anti-bodies and may even find them possessed of power and beauty. Unless an unprecedented conversion follows the advent of the new culture, nothing less than this will be the fate of *Our America.* This book is not mere compilation of critical opinions and cultural attitudes; deeper than even its psychoanalytical content are to be found "the artistic milieu that nurtured Frank and a complete statement of his temperament." These elements are held within a structure of admitted significance. Hence *Our America* is a *work of art* in the critical form. And the ultimate judgment concerning it must be leveled from this point of view.

3

In using a method of massed division in this study of Munson's work, I have inadvertently omitted certain of his units, the most important omission being his valuing of the esthetic criticism of Waldo Frank as contained in *The Art of the Vieux Colombier* and *Our America.* In this section, where I shall consider the *Study* as an art product, I can do no more than mention them, and indicate their structural placement.

The form of this *Study* is the result of an intellectual choice and of an emotional propulsion. By statement and by fact it is a chronological narrative. But to give this method, with its fixed sequences and customary implication, in no way exhausts the *Study*'s structural importance. One knows by it that the literary career of Waldo Frank will be followed. And, if its internal mechanics be adequately handled, if Frank as a writer swings clearly into view, one is prepared to say that it is a success. On this count I consider it successful.

First of all, the *Study* unfolds. It does not seek to cloak its subject. It does not seek to clothe it in wrapping alien to its nature. "Each new contribution shall be gauged by the inner laws of it genesis" (—Waldo Frank). This means that it does not commit the inconsistency of commending the objective in art; of using a subjective measure in its own operation. It splendidly applies esthetic or cultural logic. The language of this logic is sinewy, now complex, now short, terse, always lucid. And when it carries a full charge of enthusiasm it has its own dynamic lyricism, its own trenchant beauty. The *Study* maintains a skilled balance between its parts. Introductions and transitions have a well-oiled functioning. The condensations are superb. In fact, since the body of the work is but some fifty-five pages, the entire form is finely condensed. Judgments follow sharply upon conclusive evidence. Judgments are sensitively withheld where evidence is lacking, or where it is not yet crystallized. Yes, as a chronological narrative this *Study* is successful; I believe it to be considerably more.

What Munson desired was an analytical rather than a laudatory monograph. He was possessed, however, of a genuine pervasive enthusiasm for his material. His purpose is achieved by a formal channeling of this emotion. The dynamics of the *Study* issue from its control. And when at natural intervals specific passages are charged by it, enthusiasm functions structurally as accelerated movement.

After a short introductory paragraph, this movement grips Frank as the associate editor of *The Seven Arts.* There follows an even, steady progression through *The Unwelcome Man,* a slight pause in *The Art of the Vieux Colombier,* and a rapid sweep upward to *Our America.* The acceleration is maintained in Munson's contrasting cultural program. It subsides in *The Dark Mother* and is somewhat diffused and absorbed in the Rosenfeld complication. Swinging together in the last passage of the foregoing material, the movement rises to crescendo in *Rahab.* In *City Block* crescendo is sustained. Then, through Frank's contemporary placement and the James Joyce contrast there is a swift progression to the end. Here, a synthetic Frank is deposited. His parts, dissected in time, now swing together to a spatial whole. The figure is compelling, deeply vital, glowing. Here too the separate units of the *Study* are finally integrated. Thus it is seen that a double synthesis is achieved. And the book is evident as a dynamic form.

Oxen Cart and Warfare

Among those already acquainted with [Kenneth] Burke's writing, the opinion is held that his concerns are primarily aesthetic ones. He has been recognized as a unique producer of technical mechanisms, deliberately undertaken for no human work, in fact, projected parallel to experience. Therefore it is thought that he willfully slights content to the extent that content is quite negligible in his stories. And from these suppositions the inference is drawn that Burke exists entirely apart from the currents and problems of our general psyche.

Mr. Burke himself has openly contributed to these opinions and, at times, may believe in them. In his Author's Note to *The White Oxen,* the rhetorical properties of this book are emphasized. And he has stressed the "masculine aesthetic" elsewhere. But emphasis may be a matter of wish, being related in no way to actuality. Again, half-perception of an inadequate knowledge of relationship may cause misleading emphasis. In truth, the aesthetic is stressed, significantly, in Burke and in his stories. But those who see it, only, see half. While the main emphasis should be placed not upon the technical abstract, but upon the technical as utilized by Burke to effect a purpose determined by existence as he experiences it.

But this purpose is not peculiar to Mr. Burke. Indeed it is shared by the world he lives in. For I would define it as the attempt to end conflict by means of conflict. To forcibly eliminate the disagreeable and painful. To artificially reduce and parcel life. Specifically, Burke tries to limit content by aesthetic devices; he achieves a mutilation. But the content

---

"Oxen Cart and Warfare" originally appeared in the *Little Review* 10 (Autumn–Winter 1924–25): 44–48.

itself is given over to civil strife (which he wishes to be rid of). These considerations shape my formula; an examination of *The White Oxen* will establish the attempt in fact.

It is true that practically no strain appears in certain of Burke's stories. Their material is that of bare sentience, animated by a type of wistfulness, of frustration which never intensifies to conflict. While the few raw ends are comfortably tied beneath a dull existence. But neither is an aesthetic distinction to be found in them. Similar forms have been or could be conceived and executed by any literary craftsman. In short, with no conflict of content, Burke attains no unusual aesthetic. He has no need to. And this is to my point.

In the true Burkeian experiments, however, one finds significant material in combat. Sex reveals itself, only to be doused by a vigorous disgust or by a sense of the ridiculous. Whereat, sex again appears and is treated with the same measure. Sensitivity is dulled by the intellect. Most passions end in nausea, or are diffused in the irrelevant. Likewise, broken details act as sponges for emotion. Feeling is absorbed by them to the extent that it can find no adequate place in human action. Hence human action is itself arrested. But its consequences are not quite ignored, therefore. For Burke, I find, is subject to depression, and, at times, when his intellect is well off guard, he may experience a genuine despair.

Others have found an acid bite in him, and consequently think he is a satirist. He does write bits of satire; he may be potentially a satirist. But this bite too is broken. For the intellect, instead of functioning as a vertebra to emotions, instead of allowing them a full charge on it, is their attempted slayer. While sensitivity is welcomed as a source of food to neither. For the present then, Burke lacks precisely what the true satirist invariably has, namely, a co-operation of faculties in single focus, for corrosive purposes.

As I have indicated, Burke's elements are divided; they are at odds, militantly so. This division is the source of his despair, for, having given up all hope of unity, of harvesting some conscious value (other than technical awareness) from the conflict, he has yet to successfully eliminate the painful factors. But neither can Burke sustain despair. He does not wish to (and he thus negates his most valuable possession). His intellect again attempts to slay, to prevent expression. Moreover, militancy, or any type of action, tends to create the illusion of satisfaction, and allows one to escape in it. In all of this, however, Mr. Burke, though possibly more intense, is in other ways similar to the rest of us who are engaged in the (modern) struggle. In the main instrument of combat, in the application of it, lies his distinction.

This instrument, determined by talent, by genius perhaps, is literary artifice. The Burkeian forms, clearly possessing their own logic, executed brilliantly, clash with all things save themselves, violate material, and never permit natural sequences in content. Rather, their devices split, parcel, bind it, and then piece it together by means of transitions, or make no attempt to piece it, but simply deposit it within the abstract movement of the general structure. In brief, his forms (from this point of view) are aggressive impositions, whereby he tries to kill, reduce, or in some way comfortably use the stuff which existence presents to him. Necessarily he fails to kill. For artifice can kill nothing but itself—and bad writing. Nor does he reduce, in reality. For his stories, arranged more or less according to their time of composition, witness an increase of conflict. Burke utilizes, however. Not comfortably, but after the method given in these quotations:

> A man, suffering from untold miseries, can go out and plunge his knife into a wild beast, or his axe into a tree, and by so much resolve his discomfiture. An act is unmistakable: this man has acted. But he cannot plunge his knife into an odour on the wind, or a sudden memory of childhood, or a vague forewarning of death. Vicariously, he has tried to slay the wild beast instead of the sudden memory of childhood. He stoops over his kill, spies a single leaf detached, on the ground, contrived ingeniously, and his misfortunes are suddenly situated elsewhere. To obviate this, let him divorce himself from organic experience, and translate [this] vagueness into the certainty of the intellect. Life, established by the poets as a fever, remains a problem of distress which cannot be solved in terms of positive happiness, but may be in terms of pains absent.
>
> The intellect is the most advisable narcotic, since it enables us to live a waking deep-sleep, to get the completeness of facts, but without the poignancy. By the word I create, I act—which means, I slay. Man by nature is a slayer. Having become too subtle to dispose of this maladjustments by the slaying of wild beasts, he turns to the slaying of his emotions. The intellect unites living with death, perception with immunity. Let us admit only as much emotion as will serve to add zest to our perceptions. Let emotion be like gall in the blood.
>
> To find that method whereby life, pressed into firm little bricks, is handled at leisure. We must search, not for experience, but for the symbols of experience; reason and art each aiming at a formula in accord with its particular properties, its own potentials. Idea cuts through a tangle of emotion; emotion cuts through a tangle of ideas—and each, expressed by the formulas of art and thought, are remedies against the

complexities of existing. I bare my teeth at the yapping of the senses; I devote myself, rather, to seeing how, if a given thing is so, other things follow. Yet how strange that at this point, rising as I have above my own uneasiness, having found this rock on which to enforce myself, I should receive word from Gudruff.

Paul Rosenfeld in Port

In his foreword to *Port of New York,* Mr. Rosenfeld states that the works of the fourteen personalities whom he writes about excited in him variations of a single feeling. The essays then, considered singly, express these variations, while taken as a whole, they give the central motive. Now if a man were to feel some object hot, whereas I felt it cold, I should gain nothing by simply opposing my feeling to his own, or by suggesting that we again touch the object. But an examination of his sensibility would profit me. Therefore in this criticism I shall not articulate the emotions caused me when confronted by the works of these fourteen artists. Instead, I intend to somewhat illume the feeling with its variations which Mr. Rosenfeld refers to. Nor is this intention lessened by the fact that I agree, in the main, with his critical acclaims and censures, for my "values, religion, and relation" were not created by these people, though certain of them have measurably extended life's significances. But this central feeling, like most emotions embodied in an essay form, advances on an ideational background, and at times is quite closely woven with it. Necessarily then, this background will likewise inform my inquiry.

The following figure is used by Mr. Rosenfeld to express his central feeling: ". . . all of them [had] given me the sensation one has when, at the close of a prolonged journey by boat, the water-gate comes by, and one steps forth and stands with solid under foot." I accept this figure, for it is simple, and I believe that I can understand and expand it. Mr.

"Paul Rosenfeld in Port" (1924) is published here for the first time by permission of the Beinecke Rare Book and Manuscript Library, Yale University, New Haven, Connecticut.

Rosenfeld, after years of sensing himself as vague motion upon an opaque fluidity, wounded in the sense and hence groping, now consciously projects himself into a perceived world, and is, with no too great a suffering or fear, contained in it. This is no feeling that comes from harboring or conformity. It is, rather, the satisfaction one has in finding that the world is a definite thing in this: that it can be used for an inward solidifying. Once this is learned, chaos ceases, hence it ceases to engender fear, and experience in all variety can be welcomed. It is, too, the joy in witnessing one's values and the world approach a union. And indeed Paul Rosenfeld has become a lover.

Now love is sufficiently varied and universal to have been felt in some form by everyone, to have been understood in all forms by no one. Hence, to define an emotion by this term is to convey a content, but not a definite meaning. But to ask and answer the question: Love of what? That is, to ascertain the objects of an emotion, will adequately limit it. Mr. Rosenfeld would doubtless answer that he is in love with life. I should object, for I know life that he is not in love with. Mr. Rosenfeld now loves a certain aspect of American life that has been opened to him by the medium of art. He loves the wedge-mediums, the personalities who control them. The values they have erected and maintained. I judge also that he impersonally loves that portion of himself which corresponds to this aspect. In the discussion that follows, these objects will be evident. But the present acceptance and love of Mr. Rosenfeld's affirms that there once obtained a contrary emotional state, whose elements were fear, denial, and aversion. This past state continues in the present one, obviously, by way of contrast, and hence it is still a portion of his sensibility. Consequently, when I suggest that he loves an object, I mean too that he also somewhat feels aversion for it, and in stating that he affirms a thing, I mean that he still in part denies it.

The great affirmers are those who, in acclaiming themselves include the universe, in acclaiming the universe include themselves: who have a direct experience of identity. In fact, affirmation can be given to no separate thing, or to the world conceived as dual. But just as there are different selves and diverse universes, so are there various forms of identity. Taken together they constitute a progression which begins, let us say, with the absorption of a sensuous love, and terminates in the merging with some godhead. Now Mr. Rosenfeld desires an identity which locates not too distant from the beginning of this chain. There was probably a two-fold stimulus to this desire: life was affirmed by someone whom he admired (this someone necessarily corresponded to a potential self within him): the perception of separateness and duality in the world, the experience of them, the pain of them and the consequent denial, drove him towards their contraries. And then there was a cultural program that he could accept.

Van Wyck Brooks gave the idea of "Puritan dividedness" to America, and particularly to his literary stratum. It was by means of this idea, with its emphasis on milieu rather than on the individual, its call for soil and cultural interpenetration, its formula of dualism and the correlative formula of oneness, its earthiness, emotional direction, sensuosity, anti-intellection, its humanity and Americanism; it was by means of this idea that Brooks's literary stratum coalesced and grew articulate. A criticism of "Puritan dividedness" could profitably occupy a separate paper, for I believe that while it did hearten and produce a literature, nevertheless certain of its elements allowed individuals to play false with themselves, and it would be instructive to test these elements and witness their effects upon the individuals in question. Here, however, I am engaged in relating this idea to Paul Rosenfeld.

On the plane of cultural speculation, "Puritan dividedness" opened desirable vistas in America for Mr. Rosenfeld. For if an authentic American literature demanded not the genius so much as the man capable of accepting his earth and body and candidly working from them, then the difficulties were not so great but what this man, and hence American literature, might be "just around the corner." And it doubtless stimulated Mr. Rosenfeld to a testing of himself, to tentative creations, for the obvious reasons. Likewise Mr. Rosenfeld could actively, and with some accuracy, criticize the milieu, and partially at least, avoid himself. He could gain a leverage, let us say on Emerson, reject his philosophy (and philosophy in general, which indeed is a comforting rejection), and assume Emerson's life to have been unfulfilled, because neither in life nor through philosophy did he alter physical New England, or because physical New England found no place in him. And, positively, Mr. Rosenfeld seemed to have in "Puritan dividedness" a program of integrity and wholeness. But practically this idea said: touch the soil, America, one's own body, and begin with them. Mr. Rosenfeld could not engage in such a practice. For, to him, the local soil was dirt, America hideous, and his body as raw as any that has been subjected to the modern grinding. Mr. Rosenfeld was confronted with a dualism similar in kind to that which he posited for Puritan New England. An actual sense of integrity, the affirmative desire, demanded a resolution of this dualism. That he learn to accept America and himself. In part, the effort, the means, and the results, evoked by this demand, constitute *Port of New York.*

An experience, when not hurtful to a given person, eliminates, or at least diminishes, some contraction in him, and at the same time deposits a new element which he can value. In this sense, Mr. Rosenfeld's contacts with the fourteen individuals whom he writes about, their art, have been experiences. Albert P. Ryder, in creating a veritable canvas, at once diminished the skepticism concerning the possibilities of an American art, and contributed to Mr. Rosenfeld's life in painting. (Roger H. Sessions recently functioned in music in a similar manner.) More completely, Marsden Hartley and Kenneth Hayes Miller did likewise. Rosenfeld found the soil actual, and yet transformed in Dove. Denial and fear of woman diminished with O'Keeffe, and there began the acceptance of essential womanhood. Maine and New York came with [John] Marin, the delight in masterworks of watercolor. And O'Keeffe and Marin both presented the type of personality that Rosenfeld most admires: that in which the mind is grown from the emotions, in which feeling and thought are one, and which, with great rapidity and directness, projects this unity into a medium, and is indeed inseparable from it. I have already indicated the value of Van Wyck Brooks. But, if at one time Mr. Rosenfeld accepted the entire content of "Puritan dividedness," he now questions it in part, and questions it, I believe, at its most vulnerable point. In his essay on Mr. Brooks, while crediting him with expansive influence on the then formative American group, there occur these lines:

> It is regular with folk who are seeking to evade the necessity of some preference that they tend to project the blame for their own confusion onto forces completely external to their own egos. . . . [Brooks] has fallen into a fantastic dualism of an hostile environment and a victimized "creative impulse.". . . What remains curious is the fact that Clemens should have permitted these people and situations to mould him as they did. There really lies the problem. But recognition of this as the problem would have made it impossible for Brooks to represent the career of the man as a stream ruinously diverted by forces out of his control.

Mr. Rosenfeld finds in the present attitude of Mr. Brooks an unfortunate defection from former views. But it seems to me that Mr. Brooks's career is explicitly plotted in the parent idea, and that it is Mr. Rosenfeld who has changed. However this may be, I take these lines to indicate Rosenfeld's rejection of the focus on milieu, his centering on the individual as the starting point and end. Now Rosenfeld is no Kantian, and, in fact, as I have suggested, he frankly eschews intellection as such. But should I transpose a passage from Kant to read: by projecting oneself into externals, one comes to a knowledge of oneself, I think that he would accept it. Here are lines from the essay on Sherwood Anderson: "In the people suddenly known to him though the imagination, Anderson recognizes the multiple pulls of his own will. . . . What he is beholding, what he holds in his hands before him in the shape of a scene, a gesture, a history, is the very life in himself. It is himself, Sherwood Anderson. . . ." Whether or not it was the experience of Anderson that revised his mental content, I cannot tell. But here, in the Brooks essay, in the essay on Margaret Naumburg, it is revised. But Anderson did give him a sense of human relationship in America, did stimulate the need for it in him, and Anderson's soil richness made the country-side more bearable. And Sandburg, with Anderson, created a literature, a soil, and city that he could love. And when love became impossible, there was the tart acceptance of William Carlos Williams. Bourne braced against the war, hence against all that is vicious in this nation. Bourne also carried an intellect that Rosenfeld need not deny, for it, in a satisfactory manner, joined logic to feeling. In hailing Bourne, he cut false rationalization in himself and others. But, given all these mentioned, some final rest was still necessary. For Rosenfeld wished to transform his alternate neutrals, his fears, aversions, into a constant affirmation. It is in this capacity that Alfred Stieglitz functions. With him,

> "a spirit has fled from the shattered, ashen world to the skies for the ultimate time to seek confirmation for what it has dreamt amid the mechanization of the earth" . . . to demand of the rolling, impersonal vault whether the vision of freedom, sweetness, largeness of human life, felt amid so much frustration and pain, and all of the ideal which it glimpsed so fitfully, and all the delicacy, the warmth which man's dreadful social order and man's helpless brutal self crush out, were indeed merely the fantastic lights of a spirit derailed from its material course. And, in the clouds, in the heavens, in the illimitable blue, through the dead eye of the camera, it has found corroboration of its faith sustained in the desert of New York . . . above the universal decay and personal extinction the heaven-sweeping, heaven-storming gestures of the clouds declare that all which man has called spirit exists, a portion of some eternally abiding principle. The mornings of the human soul, amid the very creeping blackness are safe, immortal, fresh, with the law that governs all things.

For Rosenfeld, Stieglitz is the great affirmer.

In the fourteen essays of *Port of New York,* and in the Epilogue, there is a sense of discovery, an absorbing, a pouring out, that mark a living contact with oneself and with one's materials. From this I conclude that if Mr. Rosenfeld's true form is the interpretive-critical essay of art and personality, then he has fulfilled that early need to utilize America. But if the essay be his form, he has satisfied one demand only that another present itself. For Mr. Rosenfeld works from sensibility and feeling, from the overt denial of intellection, from the implied and actual denial of that structure which is peculiar to the intellect. His papers witness this. His prose. But the formative principle of an essay is just this intellect which he would dispense with. Nor can Mr. Rosenfeld entirely evade it. Hence, a conflict, and what he attains, more often than not, is a half-form. His papers do not end; they trail, or are abruptly stopped by an inadequate line or two. No firmly centered thought restrains his sensibility within a rounded form. Where his content is primarily enthusiasm and the literary description of an art, he is more successful. But he can neither achieve himself nor a significant literature by the single choice of this type of writing. If Mr. Rosenfeld would be an essayist and a critic, then there is one more fear that he must diminish, one more denial that he must transform to affirmation. He must see that the intellect is not (need not be) a solvent of sensibility; but that the intellect is the only adequate precipitant of it, in a critical form. From his essay on Bourne, I gather that Mr. Rosenfeld is aware of this. I emphasize it, and suggest that here too he fuse practice and theory. Mr. Rosenfeld, of course, with his present attitude could rightly employ sensibility in the lyric, or in art. But if these be his expressional forms, then his material is still somewhat distant. He must contain within himself, at least potential, a more radical up-rooting. Finally, if he is to completely rid himself of negation, he will need new instruments, or an intensification of old ones. Whatever the case, *Port of New York* exists: the record of a personality, centering the expression of an American in the discovery that he can affirm and love.

The Psychology and Craft of Writing

Writing is a psychological process. Literature is an art-product. The act of writing involves thought, feeling, and sensation; and, though a special function, it is intimately connected with the other functions of the human psyche. Hence, to understand it, one must have an understanding of psychology, and one must use a psychological approach. Thus, to have insight into a writer, writing, and literature, one must be both a psychologist and a literary critic, and one must know when to employ psychology, when to employ criticism, and how to make these two approaches supplement each other. This need is now being recognized by creators and critics alike, though the critics are more active in doing something about it, such critics, for example, as [I. A.] Richards and [Herbert] Read in England. My own work combines psychology and literary criticism. My particular aim here is to bring these two approaches to bear on the matter of the problems of those who wish to become either writers or understanders of literature, or both. I shall speak, however, mainly from the point of view, not of a critic, but of a creator, of one who has experienced at first hand the various problems involved in producing the various forms of literature.

* * *

What in particular characterizes a writer? What are the signs of a writer? How may we recognize him? What, if you will, are his symptoms? How

"The Psychology and Craft of Writing" (ca. 1930) is published here for the first time by permission of the Beinecke Rare Book and Manuscript Library, Yale University, New Haven, Connecticut.

may one judge if he himself is a potential writer? I do not think of, say, Bertrand Russell as a writer, as a producer of literature. I think of him as a scientist and philosopher. The fact that he uses the written word does not stamp him as a writer. I do not think of John B. Watson as a writer. He is a psychologist. Both of these men use words clearly, but they do not produce literature. I do think of, say, Thomas Hardy, [Gustave] Flaubert, T. S. Eliot, Sherwood Anderson, and Hart Crane as writers. What distinguishes T. S. Eliot from Bertrand Russell? [It is] the "feeling" for words. Eliot has feeling for words; and this feeling makes him an artist. A writer, in the sense I am using the term here, is an artist in the use of words.

The Signs of a Writer

A writer, then, has a feeling for words. He has a sense of words and of word values. A feeling for the magic and wonder of words as things in themselves. Browning and Emily Dickinson were in love with the dictionary. The look of words, the sound, the "taste" of words. A wish to handle them, to arrange and rearrange them. To give old words and phrases their exact content and meaning, or a fresh and new content and meaning. A writer is a creator and perpetuator of a living language. And, within limits, he loves to coin new words, and to make new combinations of words in new phrases. Shakespeare was a marvel in this respect.

A writer has a sense and feeling for sentences and sentence structure. He has a sense and feeling for rhythms and cadences. He has a sense and feeling for the various established, that is, traditional, literary forms, as: the poem, the novel, the drama, the essay, the autobiography, and so on—or for at least one of these forms. Perhaps he has a wish to produce by experimentation a new form. Certainly he will aim to make an individual use of the old forms. He has the ability, potential or actual, to achieve organization, structure, form.

All the above has to do with the writer in relation to his artistic medium. Now we come to the signs of a writer as regards content. Obviously, he must have material, that is, experience, which can be expressed and communicated in literary forms. Everyone possesses such material. There is an old saying that everyone has at least one book in him. But, practically, for many different reasons . . . this material may not be available for literary use. It must be available; and there must be present in the potential writer an active wish to say something. The more he wishes to say something the greater the power he will bring to bear on the mastering of the literary art and craft.

* * *

The Function of the Writer

First I will note the function of the writer as this function is generally recognized. It takes three main forms. First: to inform, to instruct, to educate. Second: to give pleasure; to produce and to give the experience of beauty. Third: to record things and people and events; to stimulate actions. In the first instance, a writer may be a critic of life. In the second, he may be one who finds sufficient beauty in life as creatively reproduced in his works. In the third, he may simply put down, that is, record, what happens, with little or no comment. Aldous Huxley, for example, is mainly a critic of life. Hart Crane is a creator of intensities which often are beautiful. Ernest Hemingway puts down what happens.

Second, I will note what may be called my own program, though it is not a program. In writing I aim to do two main things. One. To essentialize experience. To essentialize is to strip a thing of its nonessentials and to experience the concentrated kernel of the thing. Two. To spiritualize experience. To spiritualize is to have one's psyche or spirit engage in a process similar to that of the body when it digests and assimilates food. To spiritualize is to digest, assimilate, up-grade, and form the materials of experience—in fine, to form oneself. It is the direct opposite of sensualization, and of mechanization. It has to do with intensifying and vivifying both the writer and the reader.

Cultural and Sociological Criticism

The Negro Emergent

Where life is conscious and dynamic, its processes naturally involve an extension of experience and the uncovering of new materials. Discovery, in one form or another, is provided by nature for most of us. For the larger part, however, it is reserved to childhood and is attended with no more than a child's concern. Beyond this phase the range of experience is quite limited when seen in terms of human possibilities. Even so, experience may and often does yield isolated moments of discovery. And, rarely, these moments come with such frequence and intensity as to constitute a state. It is then that the fortunate individual undergoes an inward transformation while all the world about him is revealed in fresh forms, colors, and significances. He discovers himself, and at the same time discovers the external world. One may, of course, uncover new facts by means of old modes of thought, feeling, or conduct. This is partial, often false discovery. For it means, simply, the extension of a given organism to novel ground. But real discovery means precisely this: that new facts, truths, realities, are manifest to a transformed state of being. In one sense, these new realities themselves may be nothing more than new illusions. And discovery may be seen as a process which merely substitutes a fresh appearance for an old one. But if this fresh appearance is related to a deep inward change, and the state of being approaches wonder, then one may rightly term this act discovery.

If it were possible to glance at will about the human world and accurately see it in its varied phases and conditions, it would doubtless be

---

"The Negro Emergent" (1924) is published here by permission of the Beinecke Rare Book and Manuscript Library, Yale University, New Haven, Connecticut.

seen that the state or process of discovery is constant, that it is always operative in some place, individual, or group of persons. This glance, for the present, wherever else it rested would be certain to observe the impulse at work within the Negro in America. For the Negro is discovering himself. I refer of course to individuals, and not to mass.

The Negro is emergent. From what is he emergent? To what is he emerging? An answer to these questions will define his present status and suggest his possibilities.

Generally, it may be said that the Negro is emergent from a crust, a false personality, a compound of beliefs, habits, attitudes, and emotional reactions superimposed upon him by external circumstance. The elements of this compound are numerous. I shall consider what appear to me to be the most outstanding. These fall roughly into two distinct groups. First, there are those factors which arise from the condition of being a black man in a white world. Second, there are those forms and forces which spring from the nature of our civilization, and are common to Americans. I shall treat of these in turn.

Because of external pressure, the Negro, unwittingly, has been divorced by attitude from his racial roots. Biologically, the Negro sprang from what he sprang from: a Negro, or a Negro and white stock. These bloods are in him. No attitude can change this fact, else it would have the power to deprive him of his physical existence. But since he himself has wished to force his slave root from his mind, and since his white root denies him, the Negro, psychologically and spiritually has been literally uprooted, or worse, with no roots at all. From the anemia and chronic invalidism produced by this condition, the Negro is emergent.

Closely connected with his blood is the matter of his birth; not his birth in this generation, but the possible manner of birth of his great grandparents. Perhaps they were illegitimate. At any rate, he had been called a bastard. This charge has provoked feelings of shame or murder. When not openly expressed, the suspicion has been that it might exist in the white man's mind. Hence the Negro has closed himself and erected barriers, resistances, aggressions, for his own protection. But these things really enslaved the Negro, for, as the old saying goes, a wall restricts the city it surrounds. From this wall and reaction the Negro is emergent.

Then there are the factors which have to do with a century and more of slavery. The practice of using the Negro as slave laborer and concubine, and the consequent attitude of white men toward black women. The assertion that the Negro is inherently inferior, that he is a slave by nature. The Negro's child-like reliance upon the whites. The free admission of white superiority; the forced admission when the free type did not come naturally. The split within the Negro group due to difference of color and economic preferences, often stimulated by the white group. Disdain and contempt on the part of those of lighter color and better position; distrust and jealousy on the part of the others. Economic powers. Reaction from the factors.

The effects of the Civil War upon the Negro and the Negro problem are as yet to be accurately known and balanced. Certain of its influences, however, are clear. It freed the Negro nominally; it increased the Negro's bondage to white resentment and white fear (and, in a large measure added political exploitation to the already existent forms, while doing but little more than modifying these forms). For the white Southerner resented the Negro's forced liberation. Because of the unrest stimulated in the Negro by abolitionist propaganda and the legal paper-fact of freedom, the white man had additional cause to fear him. Nor will the South forget the sporadic dominance of Negroes during Reconstruction. From such factors as these the modern insistence on what the Negro's place is, the emphatic and sometimes brutal measure taken to keep him in it, have their source. And these in turn give rise to the Negro's need for defining his own place and attempting to establish himself therein. In a word, the whole question of social equality, with its mutual bitternesses. From this question the Negro is emergent.

But the Civil War, and the mock-freedom which followed it, caused a more subtly unfortunate condition. Prior to the war, the Negro, though in slavery, had his roots within the soil. He had an emotional allegiance to the soil and country which he sprang from. I am aware that such a picture of the Negro lends itself to poetic exaggeration, but that it is not wholly fanciful is evident from the folk-songs. Since the war the Negro has been progressively divorced from both. For a time, he could not hear beauty even in his own spirituals; white southerners were often closer to his heritage than he was. He could not love the soil when those above him tried to force his face into it—and then allowed him no real possession. He was too well aware of the fact that he could not generously partake of America, to respond to it. He felt himself the least of aliens, though he knew himself in essence to be native. He might be patriotic. But patriotism is a lean substitute for poetry. The Negro is finding his way to them.

And, ever since emancipation, well intentioned white men, sided by Negroes, have been trying to plaster a white image on a black reality—to superimpose Boston on Georgia. This has led to an over-valuing of academic study; a prejudice against hand-training. It became a matter of shame that the men whose muscle had built the South could not read

Caesar in the original. But that the image is white is secondary. That it is an *image* is primary. Because of it, the Negro has become a victim of education and false ideals. In terms of mastery, the results have been both ludicrous and pathetic. But this is true of most educational attempts, though it is less apparent in white examples. For Negroes had a special cause for their submission and desires: the white man claimed that the Negro was mentally inferior. Here was a chance to disprove that statement. The Negro would cram his brain with theories, dates, the Greek alphabet, and become equally civilized. He has done so; he is beginning to question the profit of his efforts. For he now seeks a balanced life, based upon capacity, wherein *all* faculties are given the necessary usage. He is beginning to discard the image for reality.

I think particularly of the illusion that the white American is free in fact, that he is actually free. Because the white man is not racially oppressed, the Negro has tended to picture him as existing in a state of perfect freedom and happiness. Economically, all sorts of avenues and opportunities are imagined to be open to him, so that, if he but wishes and works for it, the fruits of the earth will come into his possession. Every white boy has a *real* chance to become a millionaire and land in the White House. There has been a strong tendency to think of the white man as being psychologically free: he can think, feel, and do just what he pleases. It is assumed, among other things, that the white man *voluntarily* oppresses the Negro, that he freely hates him, that white mobs are acting from free will when they lynch a Negro. In brief, the white man is seen to exist above the laws of necessity and determinism. Indeed, he is believed to sit beside the throne of God, already. This attitude, more than any other, has stimulated the Negro's wish to be like the white man, to be white in fact. It is now being realized, however, that the mass of whites, save in the single instance of racial oppression, are as bound and determined as the mass of blacks, that the fundamental limitations are common to humanity, and that their transcendence demands something more than the mere possession of a white skin, or of a white psychology.

There are, in addition to factors already considered, several other quite important ones. But for the present I will do no more than mention them. A painful self-consciousness, which makes it difficult for the Negro to meet even the well disposed of another race. A suspicion that he is being patronized. An emotionalism on the one hand, an emotional sterility on the other. The list could be continued.

Nor is it necessary that I give a detailed account of those forms and forces which arise from the nature of our civilization and are common to Americans, for these have received extended treatment: their features and effects are familiar to everyone. The chaos and strain of these times, the lack of a functioning religion, religious pretense and charlatanism, the reaction from these to materialism, industrialism, the ideal of material success, a devitalizing puritanism, herd psychology, the premium placed on individuality, the stupidities, lies, and superstitions that Mr. Mencken has wared on, and so on, and so on. In general, all these elements can be grouped under the head of environmental influences as opposed to essential nature. From these, as I say, the Negro is emergent.

Precisely what, however, do I mean by emergent? Do I mean that the Negro is escaping or trying to escape from these things, that he denies their existence in him and is seeking to forget them? On the contrary, for the first time the Negro is fully recognizing that they do exist in him: this constitutes one aspect of his discovery. The Negro can no more leave them behind than a gull can leave water—but in both cases detachment is possible. The Negro is emerging to a place where he can see just what these factors are, the extent to which he has merely reacted to their stimuli, the extent to which he has been controlled by them. In a sense, he is adjusting to this feature of his reality. Further, he is discovering a self, an essence, interior to this crust-compound.

It would be premature to seek a final definition of this essence, for the act of discovery is only recently initiated, and, moreover, it is for the individual himself to reveal it in his own way and time. Nevertheless, I have already suggested certain of its features: it may be serviceable that I now bring these together and tentatively expand them.

The Negro has found his roots. He is in fruitful contact with his ancestry. He partakes of an uninterrupted stream of energy. He is moved by the vital determinants of racial heritage. And something of their spirit now lives within him. He is about to harvest whatever the past has stored, good and evil. He is about to be released from an unconscious and negative concern with it.

He is discovering his body, "for no man ever hated his own flesh; but nourisheth and cherisheth it." These words are beginning to have real meaning. Save that it shares the derivation and genesis of things created, what matter who made it, the manner of its birth, the outward conditions that its parents were subject to? Here it is, this amazing instrument. It is strong and pliant, capable of work and lovely movements. In color and type it seems to include the varieties of humanity. Artists and anthropologists have been drawn to it. Now the Negro is finding it for his own experience. Let others talk about it if they have a mind to.

Beneath the reactive type, the Negro is touching emotions which have to do with the primary facts of existence. These flow with that lyricism which is so purely Negro. Sometimes they come in jerks and spurts, yet more powerful than a merely modern rhythm. Rarely, they suggest no strain or time at all, having blended with the universal. Liberated from past excess and recent throttling, love and passion may now pass in joy between man and woman. Pain is seen to be of the texture of life; not due to racial oppression, only. Likewise with fear, conflict, frustration, and tragic circumstance. Above all, the Negro finds that the poverty of creed has not killed his religious impulse. He is on earth, so placed; somewhere is God. The need to discover himself and the desire to find God are similar. Perhaps that strange thing called soul, hardly an existence, rarely mentioned nowadays above a whisper, the Negro in his search may help uncover.

The Negro is led through himself outward to the surrounding world. He feels his own milieu to be desirable: its beauty, ugliness, passion, poverty, rhythm, and color. There is truth in the statement that Harlem differs from other communities in shade merely, but not in pattern. But it should be remembered that this shade appeals to something more than the eye of a Negro. He wishes to generously partake of it; he wishes to press beyond its boundaries, for he knows that neither his nor any similar group provides the range to satisfy a large capacity and keen appetite for experience. He is frank to recognize the advanced status of the white creative world in the matters of discovery and experiment. He wishes to learn from it. But now he does not meet it as a white world, for he recognizes there his own impulse, gone farther, more matured. He meets it as a world of similar values. While he is uncovering the life of Harlem, he is exploring New York. While he finds out things about himself, he learns what other men have found out of themselves. In short, he is emerging to the creative level of America.

But more rapidly than he emerges towards it, the white world of America takes steps towards him. The Negro is being studied in relation to the general economic problems. The problems of population. He challenges attention from those who are sincere in their democracy. His social and educational aspects are being investigated and aided. Psychoanalysis has interesting data concerning him. Articles about him are appearing with increasing frequency in the leading magazines and newspapers. Books are coming out, and publishers are receptive of Negro material. Clubs, societies, and forums wish to hear about the Negro. All this is indicative of a certain type of discovery. I had in mind particularly, however, the discovery of the Negro by creative America.

Speculations as to the Negro's genius: whether or not it was distinct, if so, what would be its contribution, how best to aid its growth—questions such as these foreshadowed direct contacts. And then they came, men who had rid themselves by search and struggle of what the Negro in his efforts toward creation is now contending with. Men who are relatively free to meet life in its own terms and respond to it, not merely through the conventions of thought, emotion, or of conduct. The influence of this discovery is mutual. It is deep-seated. It may prove to be profound. For each brings the other an essential complement: a living contact made from different levels of experience.

Thus far, the most striking evidence of discovery is the change in Negro life as expressed by attitude. To himself, the Negro says: I am. Need it be pointed out how many centuries of struggle bear their fruit inviolate within this affirmation? The Negro says: I am. What I am, I am searching to find out. Also, what I may become. When he faces these mysteries the Negro is humble. It is permitted that he be so, for by this act all racial factors—black, white, birth, slavery, inferior, superior, prejudice, bitterness, resentment, hatred, aggression and submission, equal, reactions, patronage, self-consciousness, false shame and false pride—gravitate to conscious placements. The crisis of race becomes a fact within a general problem. Hitherto, the Negro has been utilized by this crisis for its purposes. The question is how may he use it, for his own. And the concern is with new values.

Discovery itself is such a value. It is the first, for all higher ones depend upon it. But it may not be pursued unattended by dangers. To these, the Negro is now subject. To say, I am. To search to find out what I am and what I may become. This is the true state and temper. But it is all too easy to substitute for this, fanciful excursions and pride oneself for real achievement. Likewise can a feeling of the exotic be mistaken for wonder. One may be thought by others to be novel, and incur no risk. But if one feels himself to be exotic, then the chances are that he will never advance beyond infantilism and inflated personality. Discovery is accompanied by respect for materials. For by means of it one becomes conscious of what a thing really is. One could not touch sand in such awareness, and not respect it. Obviously I do not refer to sentiment as regards oneself or surrounding objects. Nor do I mean that the approach should be colored by the prevalent humanitarian, religious, or predial attitudes. I mean precisely this: that respect is innate in all true feeling and understanding. Indeed one may take it as a measure of his purpose. If he acts from curiosity or the desire to exploit, if he wishes a thrill, to be "in the run," to escape boredom, to evade a problem (one will often "discover" one thing simply because he is running from another), then he will find no significance in the things uncovered. Hence, he cannot respect them; he cannot be receptive of them.

Discovery implies receptivity to all things, the rejection of no single one, save it be unreal. Prior to the present phase, because he was denied by others, the Negro denied them and necessarily denied himself. Forced to say nay to the white world, he was negative toward his own life. Judged by appearance, he considered appearances seriously, and had no time to find out what lay beneath the creature that America had made of him. And since he rejected this creature, he rejected everything. Something has happened. I have tried to suggest the nature of this happening. An impulse is at work within him, transforming rejections to acceptances, denials to affirmations. It is detaching the essential Negro from the social crust. One may define the impulse; it would be premature to name the substances that may be revealed by it. I think it best not to attempt it. For should there be set up an arbitrary figure of a Negro, composed of what another would have him be like, and the assertion made that he should model himself after it, this figure, though prompted by the highest interest, would nevertheless share the false and constricting nature of all superimposed images. Rather, I would be receptive of his reality as it emerges (being active only by way of aid to this emergence), assured that in proportion as he discovers what is real within him, he will create, and by that act at once create himself and contribute his value to America.

The Crock of Problems

In all fields of American life, whether the field be economic, legal, social, artistic, or scientific, and whether it has the stamp of the white or black racial groups, there is a marked tendency, more, there is a hard and fast predisposition, to classify, label, and place a person in either the white or the Negro group. It is not suspected that there is any other possible racial location. A man is either white or black; he is either Caucasian or Negro. What I am going to say about myself will clash against this ingrained habit. And so, I foreknow that it will meet with resistance. Some it will anger. Some will not be able to understand it. Some few, I hope, will understand it at once; and I have no doubt but that the understanding will spread despite whatever opposition there may be to it.

I should also say by way of introduction that the position I am now going to express to a wider public for the first time is by no means a position I have recently come to. On the contrary, I have held and lived it all my life, following in this the practice of my family. With my family, it was more or less unconscious. My grandfather, P. B. S. Pinchback, onetime governor of Louisiana, and my father, Nathan Toomer of Georgia, just lived in the position they found themselves in. With them, it just turned out so. And I doubt that either of them reached such conscious conclusions about themselves and their racial position . . . by the time I had finished high school, the force of circumstances had compelled me to think out the entire situation. I then came to conclusions which, though

---

These excerpts from "The Crock of Problems" (1928) are published here for the first time by permission of the Beinecke Rare Book and Manuscript Library, Yale University, New Haven, Connecticut.

widening with my increased experience and understanding, have remained substantially the same ever since.

Thus, some years before the writing and publication of *Cane,* which presented me to the literary world, I had defined for myself my own position as to race, and this position was one which squared with facts in so far as I knew them. Before Waldo Frank wrote the preface to this book, I acquainted him with the facts of my racial ancestry, and with my position. He then wrote the introduction to *Cane.* From a literary point of view it was excellent, and for it, together with much else that Waldo Frank has done, I have a sincere appreciation. But it just happened that he did not include in it my own position as to race; he did include in it statements and associations which have served to present me to the public as a Negro. And since the publication of *Cane,* my name has been included among those who are also called Negroes. So what I am now going to say will not only be contrary to the general tendency to locate people in [racial groups,] but it will also disturb the notions about me which people have as a result of *Cane* and my connection with the Negro art movement. Here are the facts, in brief, and so far as I know them.

Into the making of my body there have entered the following racial and national strains: Spanish, Dutch, Welsh, Jewish, Negro, Indian [Native American], German, and French. . . . To what race do I belong?

It is evident that in point of fact none of the standard color labels fit me. I am not white. I am not black. I am not red. I am not yellow. I am not brown. Yes, any one of these can be made to fit me; I can be tagged with anything. In fact, I have been, from time to time, and by various curious confused people, tagged with all of them. . . . I have never lived within the "color line," and my life has never been cut off from the general course and conduct of American white life. Yes, I have lived within the Negro group; I have been one of them and have shared their general life. But so also have I lived within the white group, been one of them, and shared their general life. And I have passed from the one to the other quite naturally, with no loss of my own identity and integrity. . . . I have lived in America. I have lived among Negroes. I have lived among Nordics and Anglo-Saxons. I have lived among Jews. I have lived in groups composed of different racial and national strains, groups formed by some common bond, such as art or literature, and existing for the pursuit of an aim which gave racial differences something like their true placement in the scale of values.

As a Negro, I have taught at a Negro school in Georgia. I have worked in the shipyards as a white man. I was a resident and an instructor in the University Settlement, New York, as an American. I have worked for a large grocery concern as whatever they took me to be. I was in college; I was pledged to one fraternity and became president of another. I have pursued my literary and psychological work as, well, a person, as Jean Toomer. I have friends within most of the racial groups in America. Goodness knows what race or nationality some of them up till now took me to be. I have some friends within both the dark and white groups, who have known for sometime all that I am writing now. To some people, and where necessary, I explained the matter. To others I said nothing. After all, race and national issues are not everywhere and in all things foremost in life. Even in America, people cannot meet as people, like or dislike each other on personal grounds, and not have racial matters enter into it. Because of this wide interracial experience, because for some reason I can meet people as such, because of my values in life, because of a certain breadth of understanding and sympathy, because of other factors, I have not now, and I have never had, race prejudice. . . .

A person with an actual or reputed strain of Negro blood grows up in association with colored people. But he looks "white." Or at least he can "pass" for white; that is, be taken for white among the white group. As he grows up among colored people, a complex set of causes makes him want to get out of the colored group and get into the white group. But to do this, he must not only sever all connections with the colored people, but he must successfully conceal from the white people the fact that he once was associated with the dark group. He leaves the colored group and "loses" himself in the white world. The factors which cause a person to wish to "pass" for white are well described in James Weldon Johnson's *Autobiography of an Ex-Colored Man.* They can be summarized by saying that the person sees it to his advantage, not to be colored, but to be white. He makes the transition and sustains himself in the white group at the expense of a great psychic strain and a constant feeling of insecurity. In time, if conditions are favorable, he may more or less adjust to the circumstances attendant upon his being in the white group. He may marry within the white group, have white children, etc. But as long as he lives, there is, if not in his consciousness then in his subconsciousness, the fear lest he be found out, lest something of his past life come up to betray him, lest he suddenly be "disgraced" and overturned and outcast by the discovery that he has or was reputed to have a strain of Negro blood. And in his subconsciousness there is the need to so regulate and conduct his life that no such revelation comes about. He may acquire, as a sort of defense mechanism, an active hatred or prejudice against colored people. However, his life may progress on the surface, it is likely to be anything but pleasant inside.

In my own experience among the racial groups, I have not had the psychological state which obtains when one "passes" or tries to pass. I have never tried to pass because I have never had to try. I have simply gone and lived here and there. I have been what I am. Sometimes I saw fit to say that I had Negro blood. Sometimes I did not. Just as sometimes I saw fit to say that I had Spanish or Dutch blood and sometimes I did not. Often no question was raised. Sometimes I got into tight places. Sometimes, as I have said, I explained my real position; sometimes I did not. I have never lied about race. . . . My deepest attachments are those which are straight and sincere between myself and other people on the basis of what they are and what I am. My scale of values is such that the things ordinarily preferred in life, such as economic and social position, mean comparatively little to me. I have seen and experienced and understood enough of life to have pretty well rubbed off the apparent attractiveness and value of many things which many people devote their whole lives to obtain. I have seen a good bit of American life, from cotton fields and farm life, through industry and commerce, to art and culture. I have experienced the lowest and the highest types of both colored and white society. I [have] no illusions as to either the inferiority of the colored man or the superiority of the white man. I have *human values*; I have tried to extract a human value and a personal significance from life wherever I was, under whatever conditions I am. I have extended my efforts for these values to include other people. . . .

I have shown that, because of my actual racial and stock composition, I am a member of neither white, nor black, nor yellow, nor brown races—as these names are ordinarily understood. I have shown that, because of my actual experiences in America, I am not a member of either the white or dark groups, as membership in these groups is usually understood. What then, am I?

I am at once no one of the races and I am all of them. I belong to no one of them and I belong to all. I am, in a strict racial sense, a member of a new race. This new race, of which I happen to be one of the first articulate members, is now forming perhaps everywhere on the Earth, but its formation is more rapid and marked in certain countries, one of which is America. The individual members of it are not and will not necessarily be composed of as many racial strains as I am composed of. But there will be a sufficient number of these strains to produce a type of man who is structurally distinguishable from the heretofore existing types, while the environmental influences to which this race is and will be subject will further and more definitely distinguish it. Heredity and environment will combine to produce a race which will be at once interracial and unique.

It may be the turning point for the return of mankind, now divided into hostile races, to one unified race, namely, to the human race. . . . What will these people be called? Dr. Ales Hrdlicka has noted the formation of a new race in America. He has called this race in the making "the American race." Perhaps my understanding of the new race agrees with what Dr. Hrdlicka has called the American race. I do not know. I do know that he points to the racial intermixtures which are here taking place, and to the forming of a new racial type. . . . Jean Toomer is an American. There is no other name in general use which covers with equal exactitude the facts of my heredity and the facts of my environment. In so far as race and nationality are concerned, I wish to be known as an American.

Race Problems and Modern Society

From whatever angle one views modern society and the various forms of contemporary life, the records of flux and swift changes are everywhere evident. Even the attitude which holds that man's fundamental nature has not altered during the past ten thousand years must admit the changes of forms and of modes which have occurred perhaps without precedent and certainly with an ever increasing rapidity during the life period of the now living generations. If the world is viewed through one or more of the various formulated interpretations of this period, or if one's estimate rests upon the comparatively inarticulate records of day to day experience, the results have the common factor of change. Let it be Spengler's *Decline of the West*, or Keyserling's *The World in the Making*, or Waldo Frank's survey of Western culture,[1] or Joseph Wood Krutch's analysis of the modern temper,[2] and there is found testimony to the effect that the principles of cohesion and crystallization are being rapidly withdrawn from the materials of old forms, with a consequent break up of these forms, a setting free of these materials, with the possibility that the principles of cohesion and crystallization will recombine the stuff of life and make new forms.

Bertrand Russell[3] has indicated the revisions of mental outlook made necessary by recent scientific and philosophic thinking. James Harvey Robinson has shown why we *must* create new forms of thinking and bring about a transformation of attitude.[4] From a different angle, the social science of the world-wide struggle between the owning and the laboring

---

"Race Problems and Modern Society" originally appeared in *Problems of Civilization*, edited by Baker Brownell. New York: Van Nostrand, 1929. The notes are Toomer's own.

classes, clearly summarized by Scott Nearing,[5] comes to much the same conclusion, in so far as the factor of change is concerned. Again, the records of psychology bear striking witness of this factor. For though, on the one hand, there are in vogue a number of dogmas and pat formulas which assume a constant set of simple factors, and allow, say, Leonardo da Vinci to be seen at a glance, and which offer ready explanations of why, say, George Santayana writes, on the other hand, the practice of psychology discloses a surprising and bewildering flux and chaos, both in the individual and in the collective psyche. And in general, what is taking place in most fields of life is sufficiently radical for Baker Brownell to see it resulting in a new human universe.[6]

* * *

And at the same time—paradoxical[ly] enough—it is also evident that there are certain forms of modern society which, at least for the time being, are not only not changing in the above sense, but are growing and strengthening as they now exist. I refer to the established economic and political systems—and their immediate by products—of Western nations, especially of the English speaking nations. For despite the disorganized aspect of the economic situation as a consequence of the War, and as described by Keynes, it is, I think, the agreed opinion of students of Western economic and political institutions, particularly of those which obtain in the United States, that these systems, and especially the philosophy[7] which has grown up about them, have become stronger and more organized within the past thirty years. Their development during this period in the United States, for example, is suggested by these general facts: that this country now turns out, and is increasingly turning out, a surplus of both money and products; that it is sending in larger quantities of this surplus into foreign fields; that since 1900 it has become a lending, instead of a borrowing nation; that Henry Ford has become a philosopher. One student of economic conditions states that within ten years all the main European boards of directors will be dominated and controlled by Americans. Thus, irrespective of all the changes suggested at the beginning of this article, irrespective of the example and influence of the Soviet Union from without, and within, the World War notwithstanding, and despite the protests and revolts of foreign peoples, the business, political, legal, and military organizations and expansion of Western nations have advanced. At the present time they at least appear to be more solid and crystallized than ever. And they are growing stronger. So true is this, and so dominant an influence do these systems exercise on all the other forms of life, that, should one view the modern Western nations from within the business and political worlds—and their outgrowths—one might well conclude that there were no radical changes occurring anywhere, or that at most these changes were taking place only in minor social forms and concerned only an uninfluential minority.

For the growth of business and of business-technique, and the increased support that the political and legal systems give to the dominant economic practices, this growth and this increase have parallels in all the forms of life that are at all connected with these systems. Thus, wealth, and such power as wealth gives, are increasingly considered valuable: more and more men are devoting themselves to their attainment, seeing in them the end of life, and the highest goal that life offers. The big business man is the modern hero. The average man, that is, the average business man, is already the ideal, even the idol, of millions of people; and there is a growing tendency for institutions of higher education, physicians, and psychologists to accept and affirm the average business man as the ideal at which all people of sound sense should aim. The notions of prosperity and of necessary progress go hand in hand, and both are being elevated in the public mind. To have a larger bank-account, to live in a socially better located house, to drive a better car, to be able to discuss the stock-exchange and the servant problem—these are items which have an ever stronger appeal to an ever larger number of people. And not a bit of so-called religion is used as an aid to such fulfillment. The fact that most of us are just one step ahead of the sheriff is a thing that one mentions less and less. As our need to keep ahead of him increases, so does our optimism. Yes, crime does increase, but we are thousands of years in advance of backward peoples, and each day sees us further outdistance them. Social position is a matter of spending-power and possession of the items of prosperity. Never has aristocracy been taken so seriously. Results are looked for, and measured in terms of, silver dollars. Even sermons and poems must pass the success test before anyone considers them of merit. And all the while, the inner content of life is decreasing and rapidly losing significance. The inclination to prosperity and the inclination to suicide are somehow compatible. At any rate, both are increasing.

* * *

Thus, while it is a fact that modern society is in flux, it is also a fact that modern society is crystallized and formed about the solid structure of big business; and while modern psychology is the psychology of a transitional period, it is also the psychology of a stabilized big business period. It is desirable to keep both of these general facts in mind when we now turn to consider the particular matter of race problems and their relation to the other forms of the modern social order.

But now, in order to give this article focus and points of concrete reference, I shall take America—that is, the United States—as a sufficiently representative modern society, and as a social scheme that contains a sufficiently representative class of race problems. For here in America there are changing forms and established forms; and, with the possible exception of the Soviet Union, the main features of our economic and political systems and their social outgrowths have points in common with those that obtain in other modern nations. And—again with the exception of the Soviet Union, in which, I am told, the economic and political causes of race problems either no longer exist or are being removed, the minority races and peoples being guaranteed similar rights, the children of all peoples being taught, that all races are similar—American race problems have points in common with the race problems of other countries (the British and Hindu, the Eurasian, the gentile and Jew on the Continent, the whites and blacks in South Africa) and with the large number of problems everywhere—such as nationality problems—which are psychologically similar to race problems.

It will be well to note here that no serious student of race claims to know what race really is; nor do we know. Therefore the term "race problem" is a loose sociological term, which contains a variety of vague meanings; it is subject to being used with whatever meaning one happens to give it.

Scientific opinion is in doubt as to what race is. Authorities such as Roland Dixon, Franz Boas, A. L. Kroeber, Ellsworth Huntington, and Flinders Petrie agree that from the point of view of exact knowledge, the whole subject of race is uncertain and somewhat confused. It is clear that the human race is something different from the other orders of life of the natural kingdom. It is noticeable that there are differences within the human group. But it is not admissible to define and understand race solely on the basis of an obvious variation of a single physical feature, such as color of skin; and when one seeks for a fundamental knowledge of it, then, despite the exact biological ideas of the germ-plasm and genes, and despite the exact anthropological ideas associated with measurements of physical features, the difficulties encountered tend to mount faster than one's understanding.

One may, with Professor Kroeber,[8] try to understand and use the term "race" in its strict biological sense, and hold it to mean an hereditary subdivision of a species. I personally think that this is a much needed practice, because, among other things, it calls attention to the strictly biological aspect of race, it points to race as an organic phenomenon, and it allows the purely sociological aspects of racial matters to be distinguished and seen for what they are. Surely, there cannot be much advance in the understanding of race problems until we do clearly distinguish between their organic and social factors. But from the point of exact definition and real knowledge, the term "hereditary subdivision of a species" is hardly better understood than the term "race." For again we are brought up to the questions: What is a subdivision? Upon what criteria should our ideas of a subdivision rest? Can these criteria be used to adequately define and understand race? Does anyone really know what a subdivision is? The fact is that the difficulties involved in the present ideas of, and approach to, race are causing thoughtful men to recast their data and take new directions.

* * *

This being the case with the main term, how then am I to give any real clarity to the term "race problem"? What is it that distinguishes race problems from all the other problems with which man is belabored? In what real way do racial maladjustments differ from the scores of maladjustments that burden men's psyche? Just how are sociological debates about race different from the endless series of debates on all possible subjects that men are continually engaging in? In another place[9] I have pursued an investigation of race problems that gives these questions a more detailed treatment than is possible here. And in the same work I have indicated, among other things, that the answer which is often given, namely, that biological race-differences explain the nature of race problems—that this answer is incorrect. For this answer is involved in the confusion between organic and social factors. Professor Kroeber has pointed out the error of such practice. It assumes that biological race-phenomena give rise to sociological race problems. But the strictly racial history of man, with its repeated crossings and recrossings of all the sub-groups of the human stock, with its great number of intermixtures of all kinds, shows clearly that as organisms we are noticeably free from concern with the issues that we sociologically contend with—that so-called race problems are not due to biological causes, but to the superimposed forms and controversies of our social *milieu.*

The same conclusion is reached by both social and personal psychology. For herein it is seen that it is first necessary that we be conditioned by the factors of our social environment, before we do and can respond in terms of racial similarities and differences. If we were never taught and never acquired ideas, opinions, beliefs, and superstitions about race, if we were never conditioned to have feelings, and so-called instincts about these notions and beliefs, we would never have any responses or behavior in terms of race: we would not experience race prejudice and animosity. To an unconditioned child—that is, to a child that has not acquired racial notions and feelings from its environment, let the child be of what ever race you will—differences of skin color are no more and no less than differences of color of its toys or dresses. No child has prejudice against a toy because its color is white or black. No racially unconditioned child has prejudice against a person because his color is white or black. Differences of texture of hair are similarly no more and no less than differences of texture between the hair of different animals—a shaggy dog, and a sleek cat. And so it is with all the other physical characteristics that are commonly supposed to provoke supposedly innate racial prejudices and preferences. There are no such things as innate racial antipathies. We are not born with them. Either we acquire them from our environment, or else we do not have them at all. So that, paradoxical as it may sound, the fact is that race, as such, does not give rise to race problems. The physical aspects of race do not cause the problems that center around what are called racial hatreds and prejudices. This is the conclusion of experimental psychology.[10] And biologists, those who hold no brief in favor of environment as a dominant factor in the making of adult man, are inclined to agree with this position as to the origin of race problems. "It is only just to admit at once," says Professor East, a geneticist, "that many cases of racial antagonism have no biological warrant."[11]

The meaning and the importance of the above conclusion consists in this: since race problems are social and psychological in origin, they can be fundamentally dealt with—they can be radically changed and even eliminated—by use of the proper social and psychological instruments. It is possible for man and society to constructively handle the racial situation.

* * *

In considering race problems, we may, I think, for the present purpose divide them into three classes. First, there is the class of race problems which falls in the domain of scientific investigation. These consist of the racial matters dealt with in biology, anthropology, and psychology. They have to do with man's biological and cultural make up and behavior. They involve the attempt to ascertain the facts and understand the principles of human organic, social, and psychological existence—in so far as these are particularly concerned with matters of race. They include the aim of applying the knowledge thus gained for the best possible regulation of human affairs.

Second, there are race problems that take the form of discussion and debate. There are serious discussions of the race question. These discussions often draw upon the data of science, and, pressing beyond prejudice and petty issues, they also aim to arrive at a theoretically sound understanding of racial matters, and at practical conclusions that can be relied upon to guide men in the developing of intelligence, character, and ability. These discussions are frequently reducible to the question of interbreeding—of intermarriage. Sometimes they get entangled in arguments about heredity and environment, about superiority and inferiority. Too often they get lost in a maze of unconscious assumptions in favor of one's own type of life, one's own standards. As often as not they tend to lose sense of genuine values. The race-theme can compel the partial or total eclipse of all else. They are sometimes too solemn, too serious; too seldom does a good laugh relieve the tenseness. And now and again, I am afraid, the people who engage in these discussions are taken in by the humbug of education and civilization. In these cases the serious discussions of race fall far below the intelligence displayed by creative thinking in other fields. At their best, however, they do lead to clarification, and to the taking of measures for increasing constructive racial life and interracial relationships.

Then there are all manner of absurd and sometimes explosive remarks and debates over racial issues. These range all the way from parlor and backyard gossip about "niggers," "crackers," "kikes," "wops," etc., through naive verbal releases for hurt emotions, to propagandist and pathological speeches, articles and books. Debates of this type are particularly notable in that they usually repeat what has already been said to no profit thousands of times, and in that they take place in shameless ignorance of new and constructive ideas and attitudes.

Then, third, there is the class of race problems which arise from, or, better, which are the actual day to day experiences of maladjustments due to factors of a racial character. These include experiences caused by the drawing of the color line; by fights—physical, legal, and otherwise—between the races; by all manner of racial aggressions, resistances, oppositions, oppressions, fears, prejudices, hatreds; and by the occasional stoning and burning of houses, riots, lynchings.

* * *

Recalling what was said as to the existence in modern society of two classes of forms, one of which was undergoing radical changes, one of which was becoming more crystallized, we may now ask: Into which class of forms do race problems fall? It is probable, and I think it is accurate to say, that race problems of the scientific and of the serious discussion type belong to the changing category. They are among the forms that are undergoing radical changes. For not only are they in touch with the forces and factors that are in general producing new intellectual and conscious outlooks, but they are also being strongly influenced by the particular discovery of new racial data and of new methods of dealing with race. Though the science of man shows less striking revolutions than the science of physics, it is nevertheless certain that its progress has caused the forming of new attitudes and of new approaches to racial phenomena. From the scientific point of view, the whole matter of race is something different—perhaps quite different—from what it was twenty or thirty years ago. But race problems of this type comprise only a small fraction of the racial situation.

The bulk of racial behavior belongs to the established crystallizing category. Most race problems, in their given forms, are tending, not to radically change, but to crystallize. By far the larger part of our racial situation, with its already given patterns and tendencies, is rapidly growing more acute. These facts, if such they be, will be brought out if we note with what other social forms race problems are most closely associated, and if we see some of the main patterns and tendencies.

* * *

In America, the "acquisitive urge" for land, natural resources, and cheap labor variously gave rise to the problems of the whites and the Indians, the whites and the Negroes, the whites and the Asiatics, the old stock and the immigrants. The Indian problem began over land deals, and, in so far as it still exists, it is still a matter of white men desiring Indian territory for economic profit. Political and legal devices have all tended to be in the service of this interest. The Asiatic problem is obviously economic, and its "solution" is always seen with an eye to the economic situation. Immigrant problems are the direct outgrowth of demands for cheap labor, and of the circumstances attending the immigrant's economic condition after he arrives in this country. While the way in which the Negro problem has been and still is tied up with our economic and political systems, and their social outgrowths, is even more evident. This is not to say that economic causes and factors are the only ones giving rise to race problems; there are certainly other causes and factors, while the basic cause of all of man's negative problems must be sought, I think, in some abnormal feature of man's fundamental make up. Here I am simply indicating the relationship between the organized expressions of man's acquisitive urge, namely, between our economic and political systems, and race problems. In addition to the various historical and social science studies that show this relationship, it can be clearly seen if one has the patience to go over the *Congressional Record*s that bear on this subject. And there recently appeared in *Harper's Magazine* an article[12] dealing with the future of America, written by an eminent biologist, wherein much that is relevant to the present point, and indeed to the general trend of this paper, is considered.

Just as race problems are closely associated with our economic and political systems, so are they with one of the main outgrowths of these systems—our social scheme of caste distinctions. No small measure of racial animosity is due to this scheme. This scheme of racial animosity is due to this scheme. This scheme is crystallizing. The economic and political systems are increasing. And so are race problems. How could it be otherwise than that the things which are causing an increased anti-Americanism abroad, and an increase of crime and degeneracy, and a decrease of intelligence at home, also cause more and more race antagonism.

Certain factors of American race problems, particularly certain of the factors involved in the race problems of the whites and Negroes, were modified by the Civil War. Many more factors were added then, and have been added since then. But the main forms of these problems, namely, the sharp sociological divisions between the white and colored people, have persisted from the beginning of American history, and they have steadily become more and more fixed and crystallized. They have grown up, so to speak, with the growth of our economic, political, and social systems. And the probability is that they will continue to increase with the increase of these systems. Scientific and liberal opinion, and intelligent humanism, will tend to have as much, and no more, influence on the character of race problems as they have on the character of big business and on the characters of Republican and Democratic party politics.

* * *

The South—that is, the Southern section of the United States—is particularly open to strange descriptions. Reports of the South would have it that white Southerners are always indefatigably engaged on the one hand, in keeping the Negro in his place, and on the other, in prying into the family closets of their white economic, political, and social enemies, with the intent of discovering there some trace of dark blood with which to stigmatize and break these enemies. Doubtless such things do happen. I am told that occasionally it is somehow discovered that some white family of hitherto high repute has indeed a drop of Negro blood—whereon this family is likely to fall below the social level of prosperous Negroes. And there are reports of ingenious tests devised and used for detecting the presence of dark blood in those who otherwise would pass for pure white. This is similar to the assertion that some people in Vienna wish to make a blood test compulsory for every schoolchild, in order that any trace of Semitic blood may be detected. Doubtless there are such tests, or wishes for such tests, in both places. And, of course, in our South there are lynchings, peonage, false legal trials, and no court procedure at all, political disfranchisement, segregation, and, on the social level, a rigid maintenance of caste distinctions. And, among Negroes, there is a sizable amount of discontent, fear, hatred, and an effort to get better conditions. Certainly both races are enslaved by the situation. But there are, on the other hand, intelligent attempts on the part of both white and colored men to constructively deal with the existing factors.[13] And there are thousands of both whites and blacks who from day to day experience no active form of race problem, but who are, like masses of people everywhere, sufficiently content to go their way and live their life, counting their day lucky if, without working them too hard, it has given them the means to eat and sleep and reproduce their kind.

There is no doubt, however, that the race problem is at least a latent problem with almost everyone, not only in the South, but everywhere within the United States. For America is a nation in name only. In point of fact, she is a social form containing racial, national, and cultural groups which the existing economic, political, and social systems tend to keep divided and repellent. Moreover, each group is left to feel, and often taught and urged to feel, that some other group is the cause of its misfortune. Against the actual and potential antagonisms thus caused, many of our churches and other orders of so-called brotherhood and good will do no more than make feeble, and, often enough, hypocritical gestures.

Below the sociological level, all the races and stocks present in America—and almost all of the main peoples in some numbers are assembled here—have met and mingled their bloods. Biologically, what has taken place here somewhat justifies the name "melting pot." But it is thus everywhere where people meet. Let people meet—and they mingle. This is biology, the reproductive urge within man, acting with no thought of sociological differences, acting even in the face of social prohibitions and restraints of all sorts. The organic acts are fundamental in human biology. This mingling of bloods has been recognized and formulated as a maxim by anthropology.[14] Subject to the influence of the American environment, the different peoples and stocks have so intermixed here, that—among others, and notably—Dr. Ales Hrdlicka sees the forming of a distinct racial type, which he calls the American type. But the consciousness of most so-called Americans lags for behind the organic process.

When we view the scene sociologically, then, as I have said, we everywhere see strong tendencies to form separatist and repellent groups. On the social level, the term "melting pot" is somewhat of a misnomer. Of so-called racial divisions and antagonisms, there is the nation wide separation of the white and colored groups. Jews and gentiles tend to remain apart. The bewildering number of nationalistic groups—English, German, French, Italians, Greeks, Russians, etc.—tend to do likewise. And it sometimes happens that those of Northern and Southern European descent are as prejudiced against each other, or against newly arrived technical citizens, as they are against Negroes. Negroes do not care too much for foreigners. There are a number of fairly defined prejudices within each of the several groups; while the lines drawn, and the animosities aroused, by differences of sectional, fraternal, business, political, social, artistic, religious, and scientific allegiance are quite considerable. So that, all in all, it is rare indeed to find anyone who is genuinely conscious of being an American. We have slogans: one hundred percent American; America first; etc. But they do not mean much. The character of perhaps the greatest American—Walt Whitman—is as antipathetic to the conduct of the majority of those who dwell here as the ideals of liberty and union, and the high values that have ever been and still are antipathetic to this same conduct.

Just as separatism has everywhere increased since the War, so the above mentioned separatistic tendencies have here increased since then.

The World War and its consequences gave a decided turn to the racial situation within the Negro group. But this turn was not, and is not, in a radically new direction. Rather, it has resulted in a strengthening of certain of the forces and factors implicit in the form that has existed since the Civil War, and indeed ever since the introduction of Negroes into America—the form, namely, which in its main outline divides white from black. And thus this form itself has become further strengthened and crystallized. A number of factors, among which are greater pressure from without, increased organization and articulateness within the group, and, as a result of the World War, a deeper seated disillusion as regards the promises of the dominant white American—these, together with other factors, have caused an intensification of Negro race consciousness. And with this there has come an increased aggressiveness—more fight. It is no small factor in favor of this fighting attitude that it is being recognized and affirmed by other American minority groups. It is remarked, for instance, that whereas the Indians are hopeless because they do not try to fight for and help themselves, the Negroes demand and therefore deserve better conditions. There is more bitterness, an ever increasing absorption and concern with race issues; very few intelligent Negroes are permitted to be interested in anything else. Within the Negro world there has come about a parallel growth and organization of economic and professional activities, and consequently, an increased group independence and the emergence of a fairly well defined middle class, a tendency to deliberately withdraw from attempts to participate as Americans in the general life of the United States, a greater attempt to participate as Negroes in the general life, a stronger demand, from some, for social equality, and from others, for economic and educational opportunity, some spread of proletarian class consciousness, some activity in art and literature.

From the point of view of deliberate intention, it would seem that the new Negro is much more Negro and much less American than was the old Negro of fifty years ago. From the point of view of sociological types, the types which are arising among Negroes, such as the business man, the politician, the educator, the professional person, the college student, the writer, the propagandist, the movie enthusiast, the bootlegger, the taxi driver, etc.—these types among Negroes are more and more approaching the corresponding white types. But, just as certain as it is that this increasing correspondence of types makes the drawing of distinctions supposedly based on skin color or blood composition appear more and more ridiculous, so it is true that the lines are being drawn with more force between the colored and white groups. Negroes are themselves now drawing these lines. Interbreeding and intermarriage, for instance, are becoming as taboo among Negroes as among whites.

A similar increase of separatism is to be seen among Nordics. There are those who, with greater urgency than ever, are aiming toward an inviolate white aristocracy. Their already fixed inclination toward a Western modification of the caste systems is stimulated, and sometimes over stimulated, by the threat that the rising tide of Southern and darker peoples may cause them to lose control. They tend to see all virtue menaced by this rising tide. They increasingly tend to feel and think that not only their own souls, but also the very spirit of America, and even in the world, would be violated, should any save those of their own stock exercise decisive influence. And there are some whites who would like to see the darker peoples, particularly the Negroes, either deported, or sterilized, or swept off by a pestilence.

There are Jews who are more and more emphasizing the actuality and distinction of the Jewish race. They would have the Jews remain strictly as they are, preserving and transmitting their character and culture in more or less isolation from the other peoples of America.

While the Indian, still being pressed off his land and increasingly compelled to attend United States schools, holds aloof so far as possible from the white man, and sometimes indicates the white man's presence in America by a symbolic pile of tin cans.

The main tendencies toward separatism are observed and given a brilliant record in André Siegfried's *America Comes of Age.* And therein will also be found an excellent summary, from one point of view, of the deadlock existing in the American racial situation. For despite the movement above suggested, the situation is indeed in deadlock. The races cannot draw nearer together; nor can they draw much farther apart—and still remain races in America. But they will undoubtedly push away from one another, until they have completely occupied what small room for withdrawal is still left. For, as I have indicated, the strongest forces now active are tending to intensify and crystallize the very patterns, tendencies, and conditions that brought about the present situation.

Thus, from a racial point of view, and, to my mind, from several other points of view, America, which set out to be a land of the free, has become instead a social trap. The dominant forms of her social life—her economic, political, educational, social, and racial forms—compel her people to exist and meet in just the ways most conducive to the maintenance of this trap. All Americans are in it—the white no less than the black, the black no more than the red, the Jew no more than the gentile. It is sometimes thought, both by themselves and by others, that the dominant white Protestant holds the keys to the situation, and could, by a simple turn of the hand, unlock it if he wished to. But this is not fact—it is fiction. The dominant white is just as much a victim of his form as is the Negro of his; while both are equally held by the major American customs and institutions. This is sound social science and it is sound psychology. And until all parties recognize it to be so, and stop berating one another, and get down to work to bring about basic constructive changes, it is romance to talk about solving race problems. As it is, both white and colored people share the same stupidity; for both see no other way out than by intensifying the very attitudes which entrapped them. And so, Americans of all colors and of most descriptions are crawling about their social prison, which is still called Democracy. They are unable to see, and indeed they do not suspect, what it is that holds them; perhaps they do not realize that they are held, so busy are they with their by now habitual rivalries, fears, egotisms, hatreds, and illusions.

But perhaps it is premature to call the prevalent racial tendencies stupid and short sighted. It may be that a solution does lie in the direction which calls for an increase to bursting point of the existing conditions. Circumstances have been known to change as a result of the accentuation of their negative factors. But as often as not, the change, when summed up, is seen to have consisted of no more than a complete disappearance of all positive factors. However this may be, there is no doubt that race prejudice, and all associated with it, is tending to carry the entire body of America toward some such climax. Much of the writing about Nordics and Negroes, and much of the talk as to who is superior and who is inferior and who is equal, and all the other nonsense about race, is just so much verbal fanfare accompanying the actual march.

Too often the very agencies and instruments that might turn its course, or even change its character, are themselves either no more than adjuncts of the prevalent economic, social, and racial forms, or else the force of these forms tends to render them helpless. Thus our churches, our schools, colleges, universities, newspapers, large lecture platforms, are frequently just so many systematized parts of the machine itself; while even the science of anthropology is sometimes constrained to use the language of popular opinion and prejudice. And, as I have said before, liberal opinion and intelligent humanism affect the race question just about as much as they affect the practice of big business and the politics of the Republican and Democratic parties.

But no description of the situation in America is faithful to the entire scene, which fails to notice and consider the positive possibilities contained in the emergence of a large number of the type of people who cannot be classified as separatist and racial. These people are truly synthetic and human. They exist all over America. And though they may not be so defined and articulate as the separatist type, and though they are less in numbers, it is quite possible that their qualitative significance will exercise the greater influence in shaping the future of this country. Siegfried and others failed either to note this type or to give due weight to it, with the consequence that their pictures of the American situation are, to say the least, incomplete.

There are present here individuals, and even groups, drawn from all fields of life—business, the crafts, the professions, the arts and sciences—who, in the first place, and in general affirm truly human values, and sincerely strive that life may contain the greatest possible positive meaning, and who, in the second place, actually do something towards bringing about a worth-while day to day existence. When people of this type face the racial situation, they either have no prejudices or antagonisms, or else they press beyond them, in order to apply the standards of intelligence, character, and ability to this aspect of life also. And it is generally agreed that both individual growth and the development of America as a whole are intimately concerned with achieving a creative synthesis of the best elements here present.

* * *

Stripped to its essentials, the positive aspect of the race problem can be expressed thus: how to bring about a selective fusion of the racial and cultural factors of America, in order that the best possible stock and culture may be produced. This implies the need and desirability of breeding on the basis of biological fitness. It implies the need and desirability of existing and exchanging on the basis of intelligence, character, and ability. It means that the process of racial and cultural amalgamation should be guided by these standards.

We have, as I have said, enough knowledge to start solving this problem. Why don't we do something? Why do we, instead, let the negative features of the racial situation run on and intensify? How comes it that in this age of increasing general scientific knowledge, these and other undesirable aspects of life also increase? Why is it that in the midst of such radical changes as we noted at the beginning of this article, race problems, in their established forms, are becoming more crystallized?

There is the obvious answer that all of this is so because race problems are closely associated with the other main forms of our social order, which are also increasing, namely, with our economic, political, and social systems. These systems express and stimulate acquisitive passion for money, power, antisocial urges, and (since it is their nature to arouse and maintain all kinds of antagonisms, it is only natural that they also stimulate and feed) racial animosities. Socially constructive forms of activity, being less powerful and in the minority, can make but little impression upon and headway against them. Put differently, the most influential men and women of our age and nation are so committed to practices that are against intelligence and hostile to well being, that they either consciously or unconsciously do not favor and are often opposed to the use of those agencies and instruments that could bring about constructive changes. These men and women are sufficiently powerful in their hostility to good measures to prevent their being tried. Men and women of sound sense and good conscience are comparatively helpless. Essentialized, this means that man, the destructive being, still is stronger than man, the intelligent being. The destructive part of us is increasing, even while our intelligence expands. These parts are in vital contest. It is a critical struggle for supremacy in its most fundamental aspect. Thus far, the negative has proven stronger than the positive. This is the explanation that is given, not only to tell why race problems are unsolved, but also to explain the presence among us of war, degeneracy, and most of the other ills of man.

As regards racial animosities, I should like to add two other brief considerations. For one: all that has to do with race prejudice and beliefs about race, falls into the class of opinions and feelings which James Harvey Robinson has shown to stubbornly resist and resent questioning and change under any conditions. Prejudices and superstitions of all kinds are among the stubborn decorations of man's psyche. It is regrettable—more, it is shameful, but it is no cause for wonder—that they throw us, far more often than we successfully contend with them.

For another: our psychological posture is prostrate. With much activity outside, our spirit is strangely inactive. We are so habituated to living miserably, that it is hard for most of us to realize that we contain within us the possibility of living otherwise. It is difficult for people born and reared in prison to envisage and wish for a free life. We have lied and cheated so much and so long, that we have become cynical as to the existence of real virtue. Too much routine and cheap pleasure, and perhaps an overdose of book learning, have dulled our sense of potentialities. Too little meaning too long in life has led us to doubt that life has any real significance. When men are in psychological states of these kinds, it is difficult for positive appeals to energize them. They are inclined not to see or recognize good means when these are offered them. They are inclined to let the best of tools lie useless. And thus we face the possibility that we, who have almost enough knowledge to separate the atom, may fail to separate men from their antagonisms.

Notes

1. A series of articles by Waldo Frank, in *The New Republic*, 1927–28.
2. Articles by Joseph Wood Krutch, in *The Atlantic Monthly*, 1927–28.
3. *Philosophy*, by Bertrand Russell.
4. *The Mind in the Making*, by James Harvey Robinson.
5. *Where is Civilization Going?* by Scott Nearing.
6. *The New Universe*, by Baker Brownell.
7. See Chapter VII, "The Sickness of an Acquisitive Society"; *The Mind in the Making*.

8. See *Anthropology,* by A. L. Kroeber, particularly the first five chapters.
9. "The Crock of Problems," by Jean Toomer.
10. General psychological facts bearing on this conclusion will be found in Behaviorism, by John B. Watson.
11. *Heredity and Human Affairs,* by Edward M. East.
12. "The Future of America, A Biological Forecast," anonymous, in *Harper's Magazine,* April 1928.
13. In this connection, see *The Advancing South,* by Edwin Mims.
14. For a concise statement of this maxim, together with data to this effect drawn from a study of racial crossing in America, see *The American Negro,* by Melville J. Herskovits.

Letter from America

The election of Herbert Hoover to the presidency of the United States remains, in my opinion, the most important in the history of the country. Its importance was threefold. Firstly, it transcended its political significance, representing a challenge that questions the entire life and orientation of America. Secondly, it was a dynamic decision, made during a crucial period in American history. It is likely that Mr. Hoover will be president for the next eight years; and he will not be simply a puppet, but an active center of influence. His cabinet members, dominant American types with tendencies that are practical, positive, commercial, and rational, will direct national affairs during these years. And during this period the fate not only of America but of Western civilization will be determined. Thirdly, the election crystallized both the best and the worst of our national and individual character; and it showed what we are lacking. It also demonstrated what we do and do not value. No thinking individual has any doubt presently about the character and personality of the American people. In sum, an analysis of this election facilitates a complete and exact comprehension of our national psyche. In this letter I will point to only a few of these significations.

It is interesting to note that before the election almost everyone, regardless of party affiliation, regardless of social class, regardless of personal temperament, knew beyond the shadow of a doubt that Hoover,

"Letter from America" originally appeared in the French journal *Bifur* 1 (May 1929): 105–14 as "Lettre D'Amerique," translated into French by Victor Llona. Joshua Kretchmar and the present editor translated Toomer's essay into English for this volume.

an experienced businessman, would be elected; and that Smith, a proven politician, would be defeated. Quite simply, the majority of us, consciously or not, understood the conventions and dominant forces of our country. We understood that Hoover corresponded to it and that Smith did not.

Herbert Hoover is the very symbol of business, of efficiency, of prohibition, and of Protestantism. He represents a pragmatic type, competent yet stripped of sensitivity and imagination. He confirms that we have definitely abandoned the era of social idealism, and that we are ready to get to work. We no longer need trouble ourselves with dreams, with feelings, with aspirations—all positive ideals but without material advantage. He promises us a continuation of prosperity. And prosperity it seems is a term which embraces all which has value, all which is desirable. Woodrow Wilson proposed to make the world safe for democracy; Herbert Hoover convinces us that the world is the domain of business.

For Alfred Smith, the old idealism, the ancient courtesy of paying attention to feelings, still lingered. He spoke to us of a better and a more beautiful society. He was less prohibitive, more liberal, and had other interests besides business. He was therefore a source of uneasiness. We did not want him, as he was behind the times. He was not from our era. Several years ago, Sinclair Lewis wrote a book called *Babbit.* And in the intervening years all the Babbits of America have anticipated a government of business. They have it now. In the barbershops before the election you often heard "We'll see if America wants a businessman or a politician for president." We've seen.

Thomas Edison once said, "The government of the United States is the largest commercial enterprise in the world; and Herbert Hoover is the man best qualified to lead it." We did not doubt the wisdom of the first part of Edison's statement; and by an overwhelming majority we have affirmed the second part. In sum, Hoover was the man businessmen needed. His election galvanized the prevailing commercial interests and gave stimulus and assurance to all who participated in the business sphere of life.

This signifies that the trend we have followed since the World War will not change; indeed, it will be accelerated. More than ever we are going to make money and diminish the art of living. In my opinion, this trend is wrong-headed. From the perspective of national and individual life and culture, it is, of course, subject to harsh criticism, as it is from the perspective of world harmony. Here, however, I support my opinion not with a cultural critique, but with the testimony of those whose professions support this new direction and profit from it. In their daily lives and in their sincere personal feelings, however, these people reject the philosophy of capitalism. That is, they are businessmen who love profit as if it were a sport but feel it is a vile game, something to be rid of as quickly as possible. Thousands of them submit to the present with disgust, impatiently awaiting the moment when they can let it go. They want to accumulate a small fortune and then retire. This is not the attitude of someone who loves his profession. On the contrary, this is the attitude of someone who hates it. Much of the talk concerning the grandeur and glory of business, then, is propaganda of the worst kind. In short, many of those who apparently support this current trend truly detest it in reality.

The election signifies as well that business is going to extend its domination to other institutions of American life. The arts, sciences, and professions will now have to adopt the rhythms and techniques of commerce, of industry, of finance, and of advertising. Advertising is the worst American vice. Bernard Shaw once said that business is an excellent thing when confined to its own sphere. But when it is the exclusive aim of government, as in America today, it becomes an agent of destruction for the individual—as far as its management goes. And so we are at strong risk of seeing business not just direct but become the government. Soon we will say America *is* Business. Education, science, religion, philosophy, in short, all the liberal professions and forms of culture will become no more than extensions of Big Business. The majority of Americans seem to want this. It appears as well that the majority wants another World War, as well. In any case, we are not prepared to risk losing even five dollars to prevent another war. We know perfectly well that we are producing too much; and we know that overproduction, accompanied by overcapitalization, leads ultimately to a search for foreign markets; and that the competition surrounding these markets brings nations into conflict with one another. But overproduction is, it seems, an integral part of our prosperity. At any cost, we must have prosperity. Hoover was elected to extend the reign of prosperity which Coolidge and Harding, both Republicans, are supposed to have inaugurated. But must we provide for ourselves so we can obtain a raise to buy a bigger car and live in a better neighborhood without regard for the future promise of our nation?

We do not see, we do not perceive, the important and fundamental issues. And the fault lies with our leaders, who are incompetent. It is not necessary to incriminate the American people, but rather their government and its officials. And when we do use our discriminating insight to evaluate issues, it is only better to see insignificant points and trivial gains. From birth we are taught to see this only. We want to obtain these paltry things in order to make ourselves bigger and better. Bigger and better, always. It's America's motto. We already have in our hands gigantic and important things, yet we do not want to realize it. We search for petty things—and we find them. We spend our time exchanging them. It's a trait of the American psyche and a ridiculous aspect of our national character. It is also a serious aspect and weighted with dire possibilities. But we will deal with that later.

We are, as it were, a nation of builders. A crying need forces us to begin with almost nothing and increase what we have exponentially. We discover a desert and there we build a nation. We take a swamp or a prairie and build a city over it. Chicago, for example, is such a city of this type. It was erected on the prairie on the shores of Lake Michigan. There are still people who remember when the region was called a pig sty, a tract of muddy land. Yet today the city has more than three million people, coming from all parts of the world; and after New York it is the most important city in America. Yet Chicago is more American than New York. It is, I believe, the prototype of the American city. People who live elsewhere often hear of the negative aspects of Chicago: the crime, the gangsters, the racketeers, the gunmen. They hear as well about its comic-opera style of politics. To be sure, there is a certain grain of truth in these characterizations; but Chicago possesses a positive side, as well. It elevates and perpetuates the highest qualities of the American character. In its juxtaposition of extremes, the bad and the good, it is typically American. For this is a country—and we are a people—where the good and the bad, the beautiful and the ugly, the moralist and the hypocrite are intensified, magnified, and exist side by side. No European nation is, as we are now, however, enslaved to capitalism, to the norms which the masses impose, to standardization, to machines. On the other hand, no European nation offers as many opportunities to depart from the norm. The history of America is full of unique, indeed exceptional individuals. Very often one of our writers surprises us by giving us the biography of one of these individuals. And in everyday life one meets them everywhere. When one cannot understand this duality, if I may express it in this way, it is difficult to understand America. I would add that when one is not familiar with Chicago, where this duality is incarnated in the most striking manner, it is difficult to know the country from which Chicago originated. In any case, this big city in less than one hundred years has grown up over a marsh.

Our best businessmen have started at the bottom of the ladder and climbed the rungs to the very top. Lincoln was born in a humble cabin. Our best writers and artists work with crude materials, without much help from tradition; and, like Whitman, they fashion them into significant art forms. We like to plant seeds and watch them grow. In this way, we are creators. Yet we have only indifference for farmers and harvesters. And indeed we have a tendency to misuse the finished product. Here is our vice: we have no attachment to the things we have created. We create them; we destroy them. We buy; we sell. We do not value things. If we follow this trend for many more years, we will no longer value anything. This tendency is obvious not only with regard to material products, but also in the sphere of human relations. We respect ourselves and others less and less. Husband and wife, parents and children—the respect gradually decreases. This is naturally one of the reasons for the breakdown of marriage and the family. Those among us who have inherited fortune or even our culture achieve little unless we dissipate ourselves in dissipating that fortune.

The best of our feelings towards President Hoover share in the belief that he is capable of notable contributions to the organization and intelligent direction of the affairs of the nation—and that he will not fail in doing this. He also was and is a builder. He inspires us like a symbol that represents our needs and aspirations. The election placed in strong relief the dominant American type, which we may call "factual." He is interested above all in facts, in tangible things. He is literal. He is practical. He is interested in action. He is extroverted. He is suspicious of emotion. He has a tendency to repress feelings. He is prohibitive. Unesthetic. Unimaginative. Indifferent to art, religion, and philosophy. Or, if he is interested in these, he tends to treat them rationally. For example, he takes writing and reduces it to a rational doctrine, draining it of its essence. This type is composed of two principal subdivisions. One understands the world of business, the other the world of liberal arts professions. The majority of Americans can be located in one of these two categories. Those who enter the world of business have, at best, practical skills, technical abilities, and talent for invention and administration. At worst, they busy themselves, and cannot stop being busy. They waste time and energy yet do not accomplish anything. Those who enter the world of professions have, at best, eyes and intellect to reason out the various aspects of factual existence. At worst, they reduce everything to a dry and literal level of interpretation. Regardless of whether they are liberal or conservative, strong or weak, rich or poor, they share in common a factual approach to life. In the same way, they resemble each other in that they are not particularly interested in the essence of existence. In the world of business the men of this type have a tendency to become "hard-boiled," as it were: realistic, hard, and without feeling. They boast of being this way. Under the hardness of their exterior one generally finds either cynicism or sentimentality.

Some Americans of the hard type are completely so. They are cynics towards themselves, just as they are towards life. They have neither faith nor belief in anything save the Dollar, except for the feeling of power and pleasure they get from making and spending money. Our literature offers us some examples of this type. *Babbit* is authentic; but in the end Babbit becomes a sentimentalist, and you will find in him all the heart you want. On top of that, he is a minor character, whereas certain of our big businessmen are major characters. Other Americans of the hard type are soft and sentimental under the surface. By day, when it is necessary for them to be, they appear to be realistic businessmen. At night, however, they like the sickly sweet sentimentality of movies, radio, popular romantic novels, popular songs, and brotherly meetings. And on Sundays, they are moved to tears while listening to the minister. Businessmen of this type are numerous; and here we approach Babbit.

The psychology of the American businessman tends towards buying and selling at a profit, aided by good selling techniques, propaganda, and publicity. When you meet him, he imagines that you will try to sell him something, to con or dupe him. And if your approach is found to be formulated in terms of ideas, he believes you are trying to sell him your ideas. He will stay on his guard, believing that by his own shrewd method you will not persuade him without his knowledge. In short, all real intellectual exchanges with him are difficult, if not impossible. If your method of approach is formulated in terms of art, he suspects you are trying to sell him some art. If formulated in terms of life, in terms of simple human relations, it is the same. Moreover, if you have nothing to sell, you are really suspect. Summarily, his psyche is mechanically closed to everything which is not business. His tendency is to reduce everything to the act of buying and selling for profit. Of course this tendency to reduce things to the terms of specialty is not peculiar to businessmen. A similar tendency exists among artists and scientists. For artists it is, naturally, art. Nothing but art. They want to reduce the word to art. They tend to reject all that is not art. With scientists it is science. Science. Nothing but science. Everything must yield to scientific necessity. All that is not scientific they tend to eliminate. In business, in art, and in science, the mentality is the same. I must add, then, that I do not take a position against businessmen or against business; against artists or against art; against scientists or science. I intend quite simply to describe a characteristic of the mentality of certain businessmen, of certain artists, of certain scientists. What I say implies a critique of the fragmented lives to which we are committed. In literature the factual American produces a literal or so-called "realistic" novel, a real-life poem, or a drama about "the guy next door." He transcribes an aspect of daily life, and his work has much in common with the journalist or reporter. Today, the majority of American novelists belong to this school—Sinclair Lewis, Theodore Dreiser, Booth Tarkington, and others. Many of our young writers, attracted as they are by that which is emotional, intellectual, imaginative, and symbolical, are nonetheless repressed by factualism, or a sterile aestheticism resulting from their feeble revolt against factualism, from which they dare not liberate themselves. Waldo Frank is one of our well-known writers who has tried to do it. Indeed, his works approach symbolism. Yet his position would be stronger if his mode of presentation were less self-conscious, simpler, and more direct. Mr. Frank, by the way, just published a new novel entitled *The Rediscovery of America.* It is now before the critics, who are unanimous on two points: first, that Mr. Frank has made an important contribution to a constructive critique of America; and second, that his style detracts from the narrative continuity of the book and in so doing diminishes its value.

H. L. Mencken is factual, while Eugene O'Neill tends to lose control and become troubled when he gets too far from what is actual. [O'Neill] is at his best when he works a dramatic, concrete theme in a real situation. When he undertakes to be symbolic and imaginative, he sacrifices drama to gesture and rhetoric.

Our best magazines of general interest, except the *Dial,* are factual, with well-defined tendencies toward politics and sociology and demand articles, essays, and stories that deal with the factual aspects of our world. In general, they welcome the expressions of progressive science. These expressions, however, need not be intellectual; rather, they must be concrete, familiar, and rational. Science, of this type, does not touch feelings. Our magazines are afraid of feelings, liberal or otherwise, allowing open attacks upon the emotions. They remain closed to new endeavors in literature and in art, having little or no aesthetic appreciation for them and blind or indifferent to their potential. *The American Caravan* was established to publish avant-garde literature, to present the profound, moving forces of human life and pass them on. This journal thus occupies a unique position in our literary heritage.

In psychology, the factual type, notably represented by John B. Watson, has given birth to "Behaviorism," a system of theories derived from the observation of human behavior. In content and in expression, it corresponds to the dominant American type. In this way, it is one of our most influential modes of access to the comprehension of human nature. Currently, it is a source of disturbance in many circles, as it goes against many preconceived ideas we hold concerning life. Also, Dr. Watson has an aggressive temperament and is a polemicist. But this disturbance will die down soon. Behaviorism, or a modification of its doctrine, will reign unchallenged. It has the facts on its side. John Dewey is the most notable educator and contemporary American philosopher. Dewey is pragmatic, practical, and factual, while Santayana is, by comparison, more subtle and more poetic. Dewey is asked to give as many as five hundred lectures, while Santayana may be asked to give one.

It is truly a big step from the average businessman to John Dewey. Indeed, it seems bizarre to unite Babbit, Sinclair Lewis, Dreiser, O'Neill, Mencken, Watson, and Dewey in the same category. To be sure, there are important differences between these men, as their personalities and capabilities differ. If locked in the same room, they would probably come to blows. Nevertheless, they are identical in that they all tend to deal with the "realistic" aspects of experience. Their vision of the world makes them act factually and rationally.

The majority of Americans are, or want to be, of this type; and in Herbert Hoover they have found a concrete symbol. He has spoken to them practically and in terms of facts. His mode of communication was factual, as seen in his happy use of the radio. Indeed, the radio, which eliminates the human element, which reduces man to sound, and which transmits neither feeling nor imagination, is an excellent instrument in the service of the modern technical, statistical, factual type of businessman. The speeches Mr. Hoover gave during his campaign were remarkable for two reasons: the presence of particular statistics; and the absence of any appeal to emotions or ideals. He presented himself before the American people as a commercial engineer, as a business administrator. He promised the greatest amount of common sense and the least idealism; the greatest amount of physical activity and the least mental activity; the greatest amount of external organization and the least amount of internal individualization; the greatest amount of prosperity and the least amount of personal signification. Certain presidents have promised less, while others have promised more. But no other president has outlined propositions which correspond so directly to what the majority wants. For the majority, he is, as I have said, a perfect symbol; and he is remarkably even more popular than is indicated by the votes he received.

There was a time when America was the proud champion of social idealism. It was a country—and we were a people—of independence, equality, and liberty. At that time, these were not vain slogans. We were a growing people, a people of the present and the future. This has changed. America is now a country of business, and we are a country of businessmen. The election of Herbert Hoover is the decisive manifestation of this change. In concluding I must observe that this change is not a spiritual defeat. It merely signifies, among other things, that human values, the profound and developing forces of life, have definitely passed from the majority to the minority, and that life itself is no longer the province of the masses rather of individuals. I expect to see this new trend originate a new solidarity among individuals, and I believe that it will produce a larger and a more efficient sense of individual responsibility. I also expect to see the domination of business produce a powerful new mode of living. A new type of American will form—not exactly new, since Emerson, Whitman, and Melville have already existed. This type will not necessarily oppose the factual type; indeed, they will complement each other. In large measure, Americans will take charge of their own destiny.

Opinions on the Questions of the Cahiers de l'Etoile

A) Does there exist a definite unrest peculiar to our time?
Yes, I think so. I think that the unrest of our time is peculiar in that it involves so great a number of diverse peoples and interests. It is quantitatively greater. Perhaps this is due, in part, to the industrial system and its by-products, such as: the extension of education and literacy to the so-called lower classes and to the so-called backward peoples increased means of transportation and intercommunication; the increased spread of, and response to, general symbols, such as that of material success, which evoke similar reactions in otherwise unrelated groups of peoples; increased class and race consciousness; the release and over-stimulation of the wish for power, resulting in greater rivalry, conflict, antagonism.

But the industrial system is but a manifestation or outgrowth of properties resident in the human psyche. Man exists within, and is part of, general earth-conditions. The present unrest is an aspect of what may well be a world crisis.

I am in doubt as to the qualitative peculiarity of contemporary unrest. But it may consist in the clarity of definition which the issues receive, in the intelligence of the response to these issues. Mankind seems to be approaching a verbal level. Man's conflicts, struggles, issues, problems, despairs, aspirations, purposes, and cross-purposes, are more articulate. We of this present age have an increased ability both to rationalize and (I hope) to reason. Perhaps never before have there been, on the one

"Opinions on the Questions of the *Cahiers de l'Etoile*" (1929) is published here for the first time by permission of the Beinecke Rare Book and Manuscript Library, Yale University, New Haven, Connecticut.

hand, so many literate asses, and, on the other, so many genuinely intelligent people. All the main problems of the human world are the personal concern of the individual intelligence. It is probable that for the first time in history the major struggle will be clear-cut between mobilized idiocy and mobilized sanity. Or, put differently, a contest between two kinds of human psyche, two types of consciousness.

I think that the unrest of our time is marked by an intensification of extremes; by an intensification of positive and negative forces, leading to extreme manifestations of these forces.

There is an intensification of negative or destructive forces and tendencies. Evidence of this is found in: the increase of legal and illegal crime; the increased use of drugs and dope; the greater number of suicides; the preparations for a greater war; the increase of prejudices and antagonisms between races, nations, classes, and smaller groups of people; the spread of harmful materialistic and spiritualistic views; the decrease of meaning in life, the increase of boredom and a sense of futility (sterile disillusion); the greater number of lopsided people (so-called specialists); the increase of disrespect and distrust; the increased organization, and therefore the greater dominance of acquisitive, predatory interests; an increase of the hysteria which tries to meet new manifestations and correct old ones by a panicky use of law and violence; the application of science to invent and perfect destructive agents; the artificially stimulated mass reduction of all things, including art and literature, to the lowest standard level.

There is an intensification of positive or constructive forces and tendencies. Evidence of this is found in: an increased ability to invent and make tools and machines which, if rightly used, would be of great service to man; the increase of sound thinking on the nature and problems of government, education, organic and psychological pathology; something like a renaissance in the fields of art, literature, and science; an expansion of individual consciousness; an increased knowledge of the individual and of society; a marked tendency to re-examine, reformulate, balance, and unify both in the personal and in the general human world; the rebirth not of religions, but of the source of religions. An intensification of disintegrating and integrating forces. Separation and synthesis. Duality and unity.

B) 1. Does it exist in your particular field? And, if so, in what form?

In the field of literature this unrest is evident. Here too I find an intensification of extremes. Never has there been such quantity of cheap, unimportant written matter. Books, magazines, newspapers, pamphlets. Writing is a modern disease. The products of this disease are acclaimed as literature. I give a few of the prevalent motives for writing: to kill time, to forget life; to see one's name in print; to become a success; to advance one's social prestige, to make easy money, to evade or justify some disagreeable experience. Then too, writing is used as a substitute for sex, travel, and whiskey. There is a marked decrease of respect for the written word. The use of words is a vulgar practice. And, like newspapers, books are things to be read and tossed aside. In their more serious aspects, books contribute to misinformation, to cultural pretense, to tea-gossip. Less and less do people expect literature to give them real experiences. Misinformed people read misinformed books. Empty people read empty books. Ninety percent of our novels are on a par with the movies. As for the writers themselves—a writer is anyone who clicks a typewriter and gets published.

Literature is fast becoming a form of business. A writer is viewed as a natural resource to be exploited for whatever can be gotten out of him. His talent (if he has any) is like a vein of metal. It is to be mined, refined, and molded into the shape the market demands. In order to keep pace with mass-production in other fields, in order to deserve advertising, the writer must turn out each month, each year, a given quantity of written material. Only in this way can he compete with his fellows, win a market, and keep his name before the public. If he gives out, burns out, or, as we say, if he fails to make the grade, there is someone else to take his place. There are as many writers as there are day laborers; that is, in both cases the supply exceeds the demand. There is over-production in writing, also. All of this makes for a killing pace, hasty workmanship, loss of respect for the craft, and mechanical, stereotyped products. It makes for the premature death of talent. And long before he dies, the writer of genuine ability is likely to have grown cynical towards his career. For he feels that both success and failure are matters of commercial accident; neither has creative value. He laughs bitterly when he sees himself forced into the role of a literary business man. Much better be a straight business man. (Some few writers are challenged by this situation and are able to take it as a form of gymnastic exercise.)

Against the above described conditions, the writers with real talent who are entering the field, and the writers whose real talent has managed to survive in the field, rebel. In general, there is a definite unrest in the field of literature caused, negatively, by the writer's rebellion against the worst features of our time as they encroach upon and manifest in his particular field.

In its positive aspect, unrest in literature is due to a number of causes, among which are: the constant effort to make contact with the source of creative energy; the effort to digest and assimilate the crude elements of our environment; the struggle, in the midst of chaos and disrupted old forms, to achieve independently a unified world-view; efforts against sterile isolation, on the one hand, and, on the other, an equally sterile participation; the need to meet the overwhelming materialistic mediocrity of our country, and yet not succumb to it; the need to be able to respond, without over-emphasis, without undervaluation, to the genuine features of our experience when and where they do exist; the task of spiritualizing experience; the task of giving imagination mastery over materials; the suffering involved in trying to vivify and express forces which society is indifferent to; the problems of creating new forms to express new experiences, of forming a language capable of articulating the essence of existence. In so far as there is a genuine American literature, this literature experiences the profound unrest involved in all self-creations.

2. In what way is this unrest evident in the whole fabric of our social order?

It is evident in the accelerated break-up of old forms; in the inevitable resulting chaos; in the struggle of mankind to create new forms—a new cosmos, a new equilibrium. It is evident in the intensification of extremes as suggested in my answer to question A.

Yes, the financial and commercial interdependence of nations (in their present forms), the congestion of population in great cities, the mechanization of life, the automatism of the individual, do tend to obliterate what I would call, not personality, but individuality. On the other hand, the very strength of this tendency gives rise to a proportionally urgent need to develop individuality.

3. In sexual life?

In sexual life the unrest seems predominantly negative: the conflict of the sexes; the tendency towards a sexual life of promiscuous indulgence—fornication without meaning or value. We are repeatedly told that the right thing is to do away with all inhibitions and reserves, all sense of selection, and all shame—to cut loose and spend our energies wherever there is opportunity. This should, it seems, produce a satiated restfulness. In practice, on the contrary, it gives rise to an enervated restlessness.

The number of mismatings increases. The general restlessness stimulates sexual disaffinity. With sex unstable, the entire structure of our world must also be unstable.

4. In the field of religion?

The established religions are progressively failing to develop and sustain in their followers the function of creative faith. They are failing to convey an impressive sense of man's potentialities. They are failing to build up functions of real trust, sincerity, respect, reverence. Religions, and religious functions, are disintegrating. Religious functions, when they do exist, are often compelled to seek forms of expression other than those provided by the established religions. Religions have failed. They are worn out. Our age needs to hear and understand a vital formulation of the one great doctrine.

5. What is the effect of this unrest on creative achievement?

It is, I think, both a help and a hindrance. It is unfortunate because in the midst of it the artist is likely to be distracted and torn beyond the possibility of significant achievement. He finds comparatively nothing ready for his hand to use: no creative traditions, no energizing symbols, no satisfactory forms. He has no certainty of response from others, for he cannot assume that his forms and values, views and beliefs, are understood and affirmed (or denied) by his audience. In fact, he has no audience; he has only those similar to himself, and those who accidentally may find some meaning in his product. And too, a period of unrest places such strain and demand upon everyone, that each one has all he can do to keep his own footing; he has little or no energy to make exchanges with, or give aid to his fellow worker. In time of panic a person does well to save himself. And yet, the difficulty is, that there is no saving of an individual: more than one must go up, or all will go down.

Unrest is a help to creativity because it automatically breaks and dissolves many of the encrusted and obsolete forms which impede original creation. Because it breaks habits, releases new energies, and prepares the way for new feelings, new understandings, new ideas, symbols, forms. In a period of change the artist may look forward to a new stimuli. New stimuli are indispensable to certain kinds of creation. Then too, there are certain temperaments which are energized only when challenged by the prospect of forming from chaos a cosmos. There are, in a sense, the spiritual pioneers, the builders of the future. It is their nature, not to conform, but to form; not to reform, but to transform. In an age of unrest they are in their element. For men and women of this type, for those of this type who have sufficient force, for those of this type with sufficient force who manage to receive the minimum necessary food and support, this present age of unrest should prove a decidedly creative era.

C) Is not this unrest the expression of the suffering of a humanity that seeks to recapture its unity, by freeing itself from its bonds of time, space, and individual isolation?

I think that the present unrest is an expression of the basic disharmony which exists in mankind. It may indicate an increase of this disharmony. It may be evidence of man's effort to recapture balanced freedom.

D) In your opinion, does an epoch of great unrest mark the awakening of a new consciousness? If so, is it already possible to perceive the distinguishing features of this new consciousness?

A period of great unrest indicates the presence of two possibilities. One is the possibility of disintegration, destruction, death. The other is the possibility of integration, construction, new life. The death of an old consciousness; the birth of a new. At the present time, I see evidences of both these possibilities being actualized. I agree with those who see the modern world dying, and, in the process of so doing, reducing man to the level of a pre-human or sub-human monster. And I also agree with those who see a superior type of man emerging from this decay and wreckage. As I see him, this superior (more normal) type of man is one who places an aristocracy of character (complete men, complete women) above all social preferences and prejudices; who not only affirms but embodies understanding, conscience, and ability; who knows quite well that mankind is or should be one great unit; who has reason to believe that man's existence has meaning, and who lives in order to realize this meaning in his own existence and in the existences of his fellow beings. Perhaps the most distinguishing feature of this new consciousness is the quickness and the power of its response to human values.

The Hill

They tell me that what is now called The Hill was once a farmer's place. On this place were pigs. Pig stench drifted down to the big house of the Stieglitz family on the shore of Lake George. To get rid of this stench the family bought the farm. Thus they acquired the house and grounds which later, when financial reverses set in, they themselves occupied. Thus the place was linked with the life of Alfred Stieglitz. Once this happened, the linkings became so many and various that the old farm must have felt that the world had come to settle within its borders.

I wonder what the old house felt when rooms and baths were added, when furnishings which it had never seen the like of were moved in, when the complexities of the Stieglitz family began weaving in and out the rooms and into the simple old wood and farmer's plaster. Surely it knew that an unexpected fate had overtaken it. Surely it gazed with amazement at Alfred Stieglitz and his camera, at Georgia O'Keeffe and her paints and canvases. And it affirmed the transformation and felt satisfied because the photographer and the painter, like the farmers before them, were producers, producers of things for America.

One may guess, too, at the surprise of the flowers when they saw O'Keeffe first paint them. At the surprise of the trees and weeds when they became important before Stieglitz's camera. Something new had come to pass in this Lake George place. The farm had become The Hill.

At The Hill the windows are uncurtained. Each window is all win-

---

"The Hill" originally appeared in *America and Alfred Stieglitz: A Collective Portrait,* edited by Waldo Frank, Lewis Mumford, Dorothy Norman, Paul Rosenfeld, and Harold Rugg. New York: The Literary Guild, 1934.

dow. The outside can look in, the Lake George landscape, nearby trees, an old red barn, floating clouds. The house rests upon its earth, inviting this part of the American countryside to enter. And the countryside does enter, and something of the great earth, and something, I feel, of the great world.

What is of equal importance, the inside can look out—and this, particularly, is Stieglitz. The inside looking out unhindered, the human spirit being, with a permanent intensity to perceive, feel, and know the world which it inhabits, to give a sheer record of experiences.

I always see his eyes, those ever alert instruments of a consciousness whose genius is to register both the details and the vastnesses of life, of this part of the universe where now we happen to be dwelling—all with an extraordinary sense of significance, a feeling of relatedness.

Nothing for him is unrelated; even twigs and pebbles fit in as constituents of the universe. Even human stupidity, for he can see its function in relation to intelligence. An accepter, an affirmer, a rich nature with a generous interest in all that exists.

One of my pictures of him is Stieglitz in a deep chair, people around him, his body relaxed, hands unoccupied, gray hair in whatever way it happens to be, but his head poised as if it were the prototype of all cameras, recording with uncanny sensitiveness all that is visible and much that is not.

There are deep chairs at The Hill, deep chairs in his rooms at the Shelton, one deep chair in his room at An American Place, and I see him in them. This actual or apparent physical immobility is an instructive feature of the man who has *done* more for modern art in America than any other single person, who has established a standard of truth.

Obviously his way of doing is not that which we ordinarily advertise and idealize. No one would mistake him for one of our publicized men of action. No, he has the dynamics of *being*—hence he can do. In this he is in striking contrast to those who believe they can do without being, and who are, therefore, under the awful delusion that is wrecking Western civilization.

Wherever he is, *he is.* I cannot picture him elsewhere. I cannot envisage him going anywhere. In the midst of people, many of whom bustle and scamper about nothing, he is with something. So surely does the center of him proclaim, "I am," that it is difficult for me to think of him in terms of growth, change, becoming—though I know he has grown.

Quite early he must have found the places on this earth which belonged to him; and he must have recognized that he belonged to them. Or, for all I know, he may have felt he was an essential stranger on this planet; hence, that all regions were, on the one hand, equally alien, and, on the other, equally meaningful as locales where one could see the cosmos in epitome. In any case, within what some might call a circumscribed habitat (mainly Lake George and New York City) he has remained, relaxed from the urge to go elsewhere, yet never resting.

Never resting. Always doing. Carrying on his own individual life and work, helping carry on the individual life and work of others, always initiating, always pressing against whatever tends to hinder his aim of sensitizing the world, deeply powered by a sense of what is beyond, the great potentiality.

He will sometimes tell you that he feels uprooted. From one point of view this is true. He has not had a fixed establishment. What is more to the point, he is not a tree. The human nostalgia to revert to vegetable may occasionally move him, but with him as with so many of us, it has come to nothing. Yet I do not feel he is suspended or unplaced. Always I feel he is rooted *in himself* and to the *spirit* of the place. Not rooted to things; rooted to spirit. Not rooted to earth; rooted to air.

If he is at The Hill at Lake George, I do not have the feeling that he has come from New York or that he may be going there. No, here he is, capable of sustaining and fulfilling himself with what is present. Now and again he may walk to the village, but even this short going seems foreign to him, and he usually does it with an air which makes one feel he is walking with an illusion of Stieglitz in a black cloak.

He lives in his house with uncurtained windows, bare gray-white walls, deep chairs, tables, uncovered blue-white lights, and in this house he creates an atmosphere. A delicacy, a sensuousness, an austerity.

No ornaments anywhere, nothing that isn't used. No "oughts" or "ought nots" governing the running of the house except those which relate to the work of O'Keeffe, of himself, of whoever may be his guests at the time, his fellow experiencers. No ought even in relation to work. No ought in relation to life—providing you do not hinder someone else. Just life.

My first visit to The Hill I was soon struck by a feeling that came from him constantly and filled the house. I particularly remember one morning.

We were having fruit, Zwieback, and coffee in the kitchen. O'Keeffe and Paul Rosenfeld were there. Stieglitz was at the table, silent, his head lowered, eyes pensive on something not in sight, absently dipping Zwieback in coffee before eating it.

Outside, snow was on the hills, a clod hidden landscape; and to my eyes it seemed that we were four people far away from everything, practically lost in a remote frosty region of the earth, unconnected with wide living. But I *felt* warmth and a most amazing sense that life was coming into us, that the wide world was immediate out there, that we were in the midst of happenings in America, that Stieglitz had an interior connectedness with life, that through him I also felt connected.

Feeling, I believe, is the center of his life. Whatever he does, he does through feeling—and he won't do anything unless feeling is in it. Whatever he thinks, he thinks with feeling—and he won't think anything unless feeling is in it. His words convey it, his miraculously clear photographs, his silences, his sitting relaxed in a deep chair.

Feeling is being. Stieglitz can evoke the one and therefore the other; and this is why he can help people find and be what they are, why he can move people both into and out of themselves, why we value him, we who are younger than he but old enough to realize that thought and action are nothing unless they issue from and return to being.

I wondered when he would begin photographing. O'Keeffe was painting. Paul and myself were writing. Stieglitz was simply in the house. I wondered how he would be when working. In due time he began.

A natural happening. His working tempo was but a quickening (though what a quickening!) of his usual tempo. All he did was but an intensification of what had been in The Hill all the while. Work and life were the same thing, and life and art. No casual observer would have thought that anything "great" was going on. His camera was in evidence. Out he would go with it. In he would come. And soon the large table in the front room was filled with his materials and prints. It was that simple—and that real.

Only it wasn't simple at all. The search for truth and reality is a complex search, the attempt to extend consciousness is a difficult attempt, the effort to determine and demonstrate by experiments the possibilities of a comparatively new instrument and medium is intricate and it must be sustained—and all of these he was doing with and through the camera while I looked on at the apparent simplicity of it.

Though at various times to various people he has told, so to speak, the partial history of this or that photograph, the full genesis of his pictures is unknown, and perhaps it is just as well. Like himself, his photographs are explicit in themselves, direct communicants with one's feelings.

A genius of what is—this is Stieglitz, and this is why he uses a camera, and this is why he will never use a *moving*-picture camera.

The *treeness* of a tree . . . what bark is . . . what a leaf is . . . the *woodness* of wood . . . a telephone pole . . . the *stoneness* of stone . . . a city building

. . . A New York skyscraper . . . a horse . . . a wagon . . . an old man . . . a cloud, the sun, unending space beyond . . . the *fleshness* of human flesh . . . what a face is . . . what a hand, an arm, a limb is . . . the amazing beauty of a human being . . . the equally amazing revelation of the gargoyle that hides in all of us but which he and his camera devastatingly see . . .

Here in these prints our earth is as it *is,* our dwellings as they *are,* ourselves, we humans, as we *are.*

If I were commissioned to travel through space and inform the beings of some other planet on the nature of this earth-part of the universe, I would take Stieglitz's camera works along, and I would feel confident that those beings would get not subjective picturings and interpretations, but objective records, and I'd feel confident too that if, later on they paid a visit to this planet, they would recognize it.

From Lake George to New York City is not far. But from the house that rests upon its earth to the seventeenth and twenty-ninth floors of the skyscrapers in which Stieglitz lives in New York, there is a great distance, a difference of a century. By means of the continuity and singleness of his life he connects them. The Hill, his rooms at the Shelton, An American Place on Madison Avenue, are but variations of the same thing—the world he has built and is building.

The beginning-structures of this world: *291* and *Camera Work,* those manifest crystallizations of his deep resources which had such vital functions in the life of their time, which have carried forward like good blood into the living body and spirit of today. I did not experience them; I do sense them now as they exist in the present in him, as they and their effects exist in present-day America which owes to them an important part of its cultural being.

The past is a solid life behind him. The future is a solid life before him. He is solid in today.

If he is in his rooms at the Shelton, there he is. From these uncurtained windows of a skyscraper he can see the weather before it reaches the city pavements—and when I think of him looking out I remember the artists he has seen and recognized before they became known to most of us, before they were solid figures on the horizontal earth. He saw them, he recognized them, he did something so that they were aided in becoming such figures.

Here in these personal rooms of his one can sense the richness of his private life, his friendships and devotions, affirmations of this one, lashings against that one, his warmth, his clean kindliness, his humor—in fine, his dimensions in human experience.

If he is at the gallery, there he is. Behind him are other galleries. Before him, maybe more. But here, now, in this one, he is; carrying it on from day to day, from year to year through personal, economic, and spiritual vicissitudes.

Here the world comes to meet and experience his world. Here life comes to meet life. Here he meets what comes in.

There is, let us say, a show of Marins. One day I go up and many people are about. Stieglitz is himself. He talks and makes things happen or says nothing and lets things happen, according to how he feels. Another day I go up and the place is vacant. Stieglitz is himself, relaxed in his deep chair, neither more nor less himself because of what others do or don't do.

Yet no one has such a profound (and, sometimes, such an anguished) sense of what is involved—the entire life work of an extraordinary human being. Here on these walls is Marin. We can understand what Stieglitz feels—and feel with him—when he sees the place vacant, or, what is worse, when he sees some candidate for humanity come in, glance around for ten minutes, and go out, feeling that he has seen everything and knows it all.

And no one cares so deeply. Ever since he discovered himself, Stieglitz has been working for truth and people, to demonstrate certain things about life, to make for art a substantial place in America, to aid certain people in bringing forth the best from themselves, and of course he is concerned if what happens is less than what is possible.

And he tries to do something about it, and if he can't—he accepts, with the knowledge that there is an inevitability in life and events, that what must be must be that because it happens (or fails to happen) there is a certain rightness in it. Then he tries again. It is rare to find anyone in whom the two attitudes—"I will" [and] "Thy will be done"—are so balanced.

As a creator, the "I will" is stronger. "I will" and the opposite, "I won't." By affirming he has done what he had to do. By denying he has kept himself unimpeded.

This man who is living in the spirit of today will have nothing to do with the things of today that distract from this spirit. Sometimes it is a fiery rejection. Sometimes it is a natural unconcern, as if in past lives he had experienced and become disillusioned with the vanities of the world, as if now in this life they simply do not exist for him.

In these days of "great personalities," of small souls and swollen egos, he is a simple man, a sincere man, uncompromising, a quiet man who comes into the house and you hardly know he has come in, who has come into this ambitious world of ours, who exists and has his being in it, unmindful of its scurryings, its advertisements and publicities.

He has no place for what is unrelated. Others may be interested, the thing may be valuable, the person may be promising, but he seems to know by intuition what is his and what is not, how far he can go, how far he can't and he keeps to what is related to him, and he remains faithful to the high task of building his world with the materials and the people who belong to this world—all the while knowing, of course, that what he does carries beyond the boundary of his immediate aims and reaches people near and far.

A man in his world. A world which he has made, not found already made. No one, no group, no race, no nation could have built it for him. His function in life was not to fit into something that already existed but to create a new form by the force of his growth. Now he calls this form "An American Place"—which it is, authentically. Whoever goes to room 1710 of 509 Madison Avenue or to The Hill at Lake George will find certain American essences in the paintings, in the photographs, in the very life and atmosphere too. Yet deeper than the national reality is the human reality. He himself and his form are of the great body and spirit of mankind.

An *individual* who is himself, who is for those of the wide world that claim him by similarity of spirit and of values.

A New Force for Co-operation

Today we realize that both individual and collective life have been unbalanced, owing to a preponderance of competitive activities. The pendulum swings towards the other side, and thinkers and leaders stress the need of co-operation. Within the past few weeks I have heard this need expressed by numbers of people who otherwise perhaps have little in common. Co-operation, I take it, is our modern rational understanding of the religious ideal of love thy neighbour—with all that pertains thereto.

As I glance at what is happening I see no such force in magnificent evidence. Many things there are—movements, programs, experiments, private and public proposed solutions—but not this force. So it is with a sense of urgency that I ask myself the age-long question: How are we going to put our values into practice? In this paper I am going to attempt to answer this question for myself, with the hope that my personal answer will have meaning for others. Here you will find one man's reply—necessarily personal statement because, as I say, none of the prevalent proposals satisfy all of me.

But first I must sketch in the basic factors of the general condition as I see them; and I must briefly look at certain of the more or less new ways of living that are already in operation.

I have no reason for believing that human nature is unchangeably selfish, acquisitive, greedy, mean, tricky, egotistical, murderous. True, these unbecoming properties are *in* us; but, in the first place, this does not mean that they are *of* us without possibility of eradication; and, in the

"A New Force for Co-operation" originally appeared in *Adelphi* 9 (Oct. 1934): 25–31.

second, this certainly does not mean that they are *all* of us, as the cynic would have it.

Obviously we also have becoming attributes, we can be and sometimes are impartial, sympathetic, generous, decent, honest, even heroic. These positive attributes [are] manifest to some degree in our day-to-day relationships; and human crises, deaths, earthquakes, national emergencies often evoke impulses and actions which give us cause to feel that there may be, after all, a divine deposit in human nature. Or, at least, that we truly are *human beings.* The question is, must we rely upon circumstances to evoke our humanness from us, or can we by intelligent volitional means tap this deposit and make it available for the constant good of the world? My personal belief is that we can do the latter.

For immediate purposes, however, it is not necessary that we all become saints at once; it is needful, simply, that we begin by reducing our destructive manifestations, increasing our constructive ones.

That such man-controlled reductions and increases are possible, both as regards individuals and as regards large groups, has been demonstrated. For example, the well-known results achieved by the experts of therapeutic psychology in their work with individual people.

There are, of course, reservations and questions.

Having had some years of experience with practical psychology, more and more people are asking, "Yes, in the case of So-and So I can see marked improvements but is the 'cure' lasting? Is the 'change for the good' permanent?" Surely we have reason to question, for it is generally known how easy it is to slip back and lose what one has gained; and, in specific instances, we often see, or seem to see, individuals who, having spent much time and energy working according to this or that system and obtaining apparent good results, to-day seem to be falling back into their old grooves, and again manifesting their old mistakes and their chronic problems.

I myself have seen this happen. I myself question, therefore. And this is one reason why I doubt that any of the now recognized Psychologies have worked out a method whereby there can be released and sustained in us the new force needed in order that our behaviour may flow in accordance with reason and with values.

I may be asked, "What do you expect?" I am trying to answer that in this paper.

I may be told, "You are absurdly idealistic." I reply that only a severe uncompromising idealism will, in my opinion, fit the needs of these times. Idealism coupled with understanding. I am urging that we must *strive now* to achieve nothing less than a transformed man inhabiting a transformed world. Partial measures are no measures at all. A change must come in our ideas as to what is practical. What is practical is what will work. A most realistic social reform is impractical if it does not attain its object. No number of small reforms will bring about a transformation. A most idealistic program is thoroughly practical if it does attain its object. And as I see it there is only one aim—the profound redemption of the human world.

It may be argued that the different countries are doing the best they can under the circumstance and that we must give them time. Time for what—another war?

No, I doubt that any of the now recognized social schemes will liberate the force I speak of.

A new force is needed. A force which will carry in itself its inevitable goal. An inevitable force that will automatically eliminate or at least subordinate or check the cropping up of contrary tendings.

Right ideas, yes. Right attitudes. All the constructive help that can be given individuals by scientists, psychologists, ministers, teachers, parents to children, and so on. This too is needed. All the constructive help that can be given social groups and nations by their leaders. Yes, needed. But from the condition of the world to-day we must conclude that these forms of help are not enough. So I repeat, a new force is our main great need.

This force should fulfill, among others, the following five requirements:

It must give us a constant sense and feeling that we are human beings—a human awareness, a *being* consciousness—so that we may expand to our normal statures, so that we are no longer shrunken, constricted, and distorted by notions of limitation, such, for example, as notions of oneself, notions of race, class, nation, religion. Everything depends upon this.

It must energise us with an understanding that there is meaning in life, that existence has purpose, and that to fulfill this purpose is worthy of our greatest efforts, our deepest sufferings.

It must give us an inner conviction that to sacrifice lesser for greater values is for our good, so that we will not fear losing the small things of life because we will know that the large things are for us, are possible of attainment.

It must make us profoundly ashamed and uncomfortable if, for any motive, we temporarily fail to try to live according to our highest values.

It must liberate us from our personal prisons, each one from his own egotism, so that each person can flow out and put himself in the place of another, so that all realize that we are human beings on this planet, inevitably together, bound to mutually affect each other for good or bad in a general condition wherein no one can succeed if all fail.

A large order? Yes—but only a large order will meet the needs of these times. Small orders are not enough. To manipulate money, trade . . . to increase buying-power . . . to substitute nationalism for internationalism, or vice versa . . . to make intelligent though not basic changes in the educational system . . . to talk . . . to write books . . . to relieve someone of a toothache or a neurosis . . . yes, good—but not enough.

I happened to experience, once in my life, a force which fulfilled the five requirements. It gave me a sense and feeling of my *humanbeingness.* It made me know that there is a profound meaning in life. It gave me an inner conviction that I must, and that I would deeply profit by, letting go of all non-essentials and devoting my existence to the realisation of essential aims. It made me ashamed of the way in which I had trifled with life, ashamed of all the unbecoming properties in me, such as fear, egotism, etc. And I was forced out of my ego-prison; I became, for this time (like the opening of the symbolic lotus), the *being* I had never before known myself to be; I felt and contacted other people with a new feeling in an entirely new way, a (strangely enough) *objective* way, so that I felt profoundly responsible not only for the right conduct of my own life, but also for the right conduct of all lives.

In this state I *had* to co-operate impartially with others, with never a thought or a desire for my personal gain. Indeed my personal self was (apparently) non-existent.

One of the amazing things was that in this experience which some would call "very subjective" I was more objective than I had ever thought possible. I cannot "prove" it but I am fairly certain that what was happening in my subconsciousness is the real consciousness, and that, paradoxical though it sounds, what is most subjective, that is, most interior, is by rights and nature the most objective, namely, the part that really belongs in the world, that really is connected with the world, with other people, with reality.

True, the experience occurred but once. But what can happen once can happen again and again. Moreover, the effects of it are still with me, constantly influencing my sense of what is possible, continually manifesting in more ways than I can write of.

True also, it occurred to me. But what can happen to me can happen to others. I am sure it has happened to others—it, or some similar experience, as we all have the same basic nature and the happenings, they are seldom recorded. Owing to fear of being called queer or egotistical, we have built up inhibitions about such things; and thus the human world loses one means of knowing of what is possible. Strange creatures that we are, we feel quite free to pool our petty or negative experiences, quite restrained at giving our great experiences. (Much of contemporary literature is a vivid example of just this strangeness.)

But to return . . . for certain reasons I believe the experience to have been, let us call it an awakening of conscience—obviously not the conscience that is built up in one's personality owing to ethical training from the outside, but the conscience that exists in one's essence, owing to what cause I surely do not know.

While the experience lasted I felt that there lived in me, wide awake, a dynamic super-conscience, an inevitable, right-flowing force that *made* me, whether I would or wouldn't, behave in a corresponding way. Here in reality was something in my very nature that was stronger than any and all of my negative forces. Here then, for me personally, was a profound cure for a profound trouble. Here was my irresistible power for co-operation, one human being with other human beings.

I believe that this kind of conscience is the lever of co-operation. It is more certain and more constant than love. It can operate where love does not exist. It goes beyond blood, race, nationality and religion and is truly universal. It is a power behind the fellowship of mutual work, of similar occupation. It can blend itself with every kind of constructive activity. It can pervade all kinds of human relationships.

If conscience is active we can and must co-operate, not alone because of ideas or of good intentions or of enlightened will, but because of a relentless inner necessity. This is why I believe that conscience is the new force the world needs, the force that will make education effective and give power to understanding.

Suppose, then, that hidden away in the interior of all of us there is this essence-conscience. At once we see the possibilities, and at once we see reason for real hope.

If it is there, it can be discovered. If it is discovered, liberated, and utilized so that it flows in the lives of individuals and of groups, then I feel confident that we will be on our way to create on earth a world-community suitable for the life-processes of human beings.

Moreover, if it is there, then other similarly potent forces are likewise likely to be there, deep down in the largely unexplored regions of the human soul. The question is, how to get at them and render them available. By what intelligent method or methods?

Perhaps the answer to this question will evolve from the interworkings and mutual contributions of all our various constructive contemporary modes of thought, effort, and experiment. Perhaps it will be worked out mainly by psychology, psychology expanding and deepening until it becomes a sort of world-science, the psychology of the future becoming, in effect, a religion of understanding. Perhaps a new vital pure religion for these times will arise, and in the world which it will attempt to build, economics, politics, science, etc., will take their appropriate subordinate places and functions in an essentially religious whole.

I incline towards this last possibility, for I am reminded that the genuine religions of the past have always addressed themselves to mankind's potentialities, have always aimed to evoke the forces of the divine deposit in human nature, to purify and increase these forces, to give them symbols, to provide customs and ceremonies, dances, music, and other forms of ordered expression and discipline, all tending towards the unified and perfected life of man on earth. I incline towards it, but I do not insist upon it. I am mainly interested in the function, not at all interested in what it is labelled. I am concerned with the need and with the method. A way of life that will energise the essence-part of us.

Present-day religion is not doing it, this is sure. Present-day religion has lost its regenerative power; it is a system of beliefs but no longer a system of forces; it is a social institution on a par with schools and community-centres. Those who desire being, those who desire high mental and emotional adventures have left the churches in favour of art, literature, economics, psychology, science. But, as I have pointed out, neither do science or economics perform the profound service of transforming us. And now I ask myself, why should they? Why demand of them or expect that they forgo their present spheres and take over the function of religion? The more I think of it the more I say No.

This too is one of our troubles. Because we have no vital religion for these times, this is why we have, to some extent, transferred the energies and the aims which rightfully belong to religion and fastened them on to science, to economics, to political and social movements and programs—where they do not belong, thus causing a confusion of functions. Again we need to be counselled to render unto Caesar what is Caesar's, unto God what is God's.

Science is science—and we should not make a religion of it, as so many who are interested in or impressed by the results of science are prone to do. Economics is economics—and we should not try to make a religion of it, as so many nowadays are prone to do. Politics is politics—and it is not right or good that political organizations such as the Fascists and the Nazis become religions because even though they do effect impressive energisations, their aims are not religious; neither are their results.

So what, then? According to what has been said in this paper, the answer is now obvious. Only a new vital religion will evoke from us a new force for co-operation, conscience, the transforming powers of human nature. A world-religion, complete enough to include all peoples, true enough to strike deep root-energies sufficiently empowered to unify each individual in himself, to bind us together by the realisation of our common condition and our common goal, to move us towards that goal with faith and nobility and a sense of a great purpose which unites us.

Why I Entered the Gurdjieff Work

One day I was told that an English editor and writer named Orage had arrived in New York to prepare for the arrival of a man named Gurdjieff. Neither name meant a thing to me, but I asked questions. Gurdjieff, I learned, was the founder of an institute for the harmonious development of man. He had once been Ouspensky's teacher. The institute was located in France. Now he was on his way to America with a number of his pupils. I had read Ouspensky's *Tertium Organum.* Gurdjieff, Ouspensky's teacher, coming to New York? I became interested at once.

Shortly after hearing this news there came into my hands a pamphlet entitled: *G. Gurdjieff's Institute for the Harmonious Development of Man.* I began reading it. The first words made me feel that I was close to what I sought. I read with eagerness. I read with glow. I gave cries of joy as I came upon statement after statement that said what I wanted to hear said. Here it was. This was it. At last I had come upon something that "spoke to my condition." At last I had found a knowledge of man that spoke, I felt, not to my condition alone but to the condition of all people who had any psychological understanding of themselves and any realization of the need to be helped by those possessing a greater understanding. I talked of nothing else. I dreamed of nothing else, save to become a member of the Institute and begin actual work.

"Why I Entered the Gurdjieff Work" (1941) is published here for the first time by permission of the Beinecke Rare Book and Manuscript Library, Yale University, New Haven, Connecticut.

* * *

Gurdjieff and his pupils arrived. Public demonstrations were given of varied aspects of the Institute's program of training. To my mind they were amazing events that satisfied and exceeded anything that I could have asked for. I was in the audience but I saw and felt what went on as if I were already one of the participants. The performances began at theater time and continued on and on as though the pupils were capable of endless endurance. By twelve o'clock most of the onlookers had left. The demonstrations continued. I stayed to the very last, for I was endlessly fascinated and would have been happy had the program gone on through the night, every night.

There were demonstrations of gymnastic exercises. In past years I had practiced both Swedish and German gymnastics. More recently I had learned some of the exercises worked out by F. Matthias Alexander for the conscious control of the individual. Not anywhere at any time had I come upon exercises that, to my way of thinking and feeling, were comparable to these shown by Gurdjieff's pupils. These seemed to take hold of the body and literally re-create it. To see them being done made me want to do them. Nor was their appeal limited to the physical. To me they were strangely beautiful, and, in a way I could not explain, profound. No mere manual motions, these. They involved the whole man, I felt sure, and were means in the service of an essentially religious aim.

There were dances and sacred dances. From time to time I had seen a number of the individual dancers, and the groups and ballets that came to New York. Never had I witnessed dancing like this. It seemed of a different category, of another world. One dance in particular, a dance called "The Initiation of a Priestess," impressed me as being simply marvelous. It was pure religion. I felt I would want to become a member of the Institute if for no other reason than to learn and take part in this dance.

There was music. It was a powerful, dynamic, deeply moving music that touched chords of my being and seemed to awaken an ancient memory of a music I had once known, a life I had once lived, a world that had been mine and that I had left and forgotten. It made me feel as a wayfarer who was being recalled to his rightful way and destiny. It made me feel that all of us were as wayfarers who had gone astray and become lost, and I felt sorrow, pity, yearning, and then I was gathered into an irresistible march. It was a majestic march. It was a march of men. It was a march of resurrected people aware of their worth and dignity and the part they played in the noble procession of the universe.

Orage gave expositions of the ideas. Gurdjieff's total body of knowledge began to unfold. It was a most extraordinary body. Man and the world were gradually revealed in a light not to be found in modern science, not to be found in the sacred books of the East, not to be anywhere, so far as I knew, other than in this Gurdjieff work. Here was food for those vitally concerned to understand the answers to such questions as these. What is the world? Are there cosmic laws? Are there laws which apply to the psychological as well as to the physical universe? What is man's relation to the world? What is man? What are the chief components of the total human being? What is the human norm? What are we basically up against? What can man do? What are our possible attainments? How can we do what it is possible for us to do? What preliminary understandings, what initial methods of training, are indispensable if we would make a real beginning of the work of man?

I met Orage and had several talks with him. From certain things he said I was pretty sure that he knew and practiced methods in addition to those shown to the general public at these demonstrations. I will always remember the light that suddenly came from him when, after discussing the sufficiently terrible plight of man, he ended with these words—"Yes, but there is a way out." That was just what I wanted to hear, in just so many words, from him. I myself was intuitively certain there was a way out; but I wanted it said by someone who impressed me as having found it.

I watched Gurdjieff. Said I to myself—There is a man, if ever I have seen one. He seemed to have everything that could be asked of a developed human being, a teacher, a master. Knowledge, integration, many-sidedness, power—in fact he had a bit too much power for my comfort.

In addition to all the rest, there was an over-all impression. Each thing that was done was part of a whole. The exercises, the dances, the music, the ideas, each in their different ways said essentially the same thing. Each, through different approaches, impressed the same message on the heart. All together they evoked a life and a world that seemed utterly native to me. Here, without doubt, was a religion of training. Here was discipline, an invitation to conscious experiment, a flexible and complete system, a life and a way to which I felt I could dedicate my whole mind and heart and body and strength.

One would think, then, that I was quite set to ask to become a member of the Institute without further delay. Strange as it may seem, I did no such thing. I held back. Gurdjieff's power disturbed me. I was not sure of it, and I wanted to be sure before I placed myself wholly in his hands. This, at any rate, was how I explained it to myself. Then there were other reasons which we need not go into. It is enough to say that I did something that surprised everyone except the one person who knew the intimate facts of my personal life. I left New York. While the demonstrations were still going on I left New York and went to another part of the country. There some further things happened, and I was completely made ready.

The plain truth, I realized later, was this. Despite what I had been through, despite the understandings that had come to me, there was still lodged in my psyche a deep-seated unwillingness to put my life under the direction of anyone other than myself, and a stubborn belief that I could make my way on my own, aided by such help as I would receive in the course of ordinary life. So-called independence, so-called self-reliance and belief in myself, were this strong, still. By leaving New York, by breaking the connections that had begun to be formed between myself and the Institute, I gave myself another, and, as it proved, a final try at making an extraordinary grade without having extraordinary help.

Now what would I do? Circumstances supplied a partial answer. Certain things I had to do and wanted to do. By digging into myself I supplied the rest of the answer. An idea expressed in one of my notes came back to me. One's highest gift should be utilized until one has attained a faculty that is higher than it. It seemed to me that if I possessed any gift at all it was that of psychological thinking and understanding, and so I proposed to exercise it, now, intensively, hoping that I might thereby develop the "new and particular 'inertias'" referred to in the prospectus of the Institute.

Essays on Quaker Religious Philosophy

Why I Joined the Society of Friends

When a man acts, he is usually under the impression that only his conscious self is doing it, and only for the reasons he has in mind. In retrospect, however, other influences may come to light and he may see that these had a greater bearing on his life, and on the lives of those around him, than his conscious motives. He may recognize that his actions had led to experiences more meaningful than he foresaw, and were in effect steps in the progressive unfolding of a design.

Why did we move to Bucks County? Our conscious reasons had nothing to do with Quakers. Yet, as we can see now, our factual and spiritual membership in the Society of Friends is by all odds the most important result of that move.

Why, as we inhabited our new home, did both my wife and I feel drawn to meet with people of the community in worship services? This was a new desire. Both of us had an individual type of religion; neither had been a churchgoer. I had felt that the church was more reactionary than forward-moving. The power radically to change lives seemed to have departed from it. Yet here we were now desiring to participate in group devotion.

Several rural churches were nearby. Also, as we had learned, there was a Quaker meeting. Our interest in it sprang partly from the idea that Quaker services were different from others. Quakers assembled, I had been told, for silent prayer and waiting for the spirit to move them. This

"Why I Joined the Society of Friends" (1941) is published here for the first time by permission of the Beinecke Rare Book and Manuscript Library, Yale University, New Haven, Connecticut.

appealed to me because I practiced meditation. Years before I had read a brief account of George Fox that impressed me. I had heard of the Quaker reputation for practicing what they preach. A friend of mine had worked with a Quaker group doing relief work in Europe after the first World War. These few scattered impressions may or may not account for our being attracted to the Quaker meeting more than to the other churches.

We knew nothing of the actual procedure of a Friends' meeting. We had no assurance that outsiders would be welcome. We hesitated. At just this time, seemingly by chance, my wife made a new acquaintance. At a local market she fell to chatting about fish with another housewife. The new friend proved to be a member of Buckingham Meeting. Thus the way opened, and it opened to far more than we anticipated.

Buckingham welcomed us. Buckingham gave us an excellent introduction to the meeting for worship. We attended regularly, with increasing appreciation of this opportunity for group prayer and silent seeking, free from outward distractions and the bobbing up and down of the body. It was not long before we felt we belonged in this type of worship. I had the feeling that I had belonged in it before I found it. In time, several members of meeting expressed to us their sense that we belonged. This strengthened the invisible links. Spiritually we began joining the Society of Friends with our first experience of Quaker worship.

We might have continued attending the meeting for worship indefinitely, satisfied with spiritual participation, had it not dawned upon us that there were responsibilities that we were not sufficiently sharing. We became members of the monthly meeting so as more fully to contribute to a religious body from whom we were receiving so much.

Prior to coming in contact with Friends I had been convinced that God is both immanent and transcendent, and that the purpose of man's life is to grow up to God; that within man there is a wonderful power that can transform him, lift him into new birth; that we have it in us to rise to a life wherein brotherhood is manifest and war impossible. Friends' testimonies confirmed and enriched my faith. What I particularly desired were additional practices, more effective means of attainment. My first "convincement" was that the meeting for worship is such a means. My second was that the meeting for business can also be such a means. My third, coming after wider experience of the Society past and present, was the overall convincement that the faith and practice of the Friends constitute, at heart, a vital and transforming religion.

My seeking and searching began anew after coming in contact with the Society, as my eyes opened to the Quaker treasure. The richness and meaning of the Friends' religion was not handed to me. You have to dig for it. I am still digging.

And I have before my eyes this vision: In seventeenth-century England, numbers of people, drawn from all levels of society, experienced the workings of God in man. They know the truth that the divine can invade the human. They became regenerated and were able to touch the springs of regeneration in others. It happened then, so why not now? Is there any other way of salvation for mankind? The more starkly I see the human situation the more urgent is my conviction that nothing less than a radically changed life, wrought by suprapersonal love and light, will enable us to resolve the terrific problems we have brought on ourselves and to advance a decisive step towards our true destiny.

The Message of Quakerism

The Friends' faith and practice is a way to God. Indeed, the message of Quakerism is that there is that of God in every man. Indeed, the message is the immediacy of God. Indeed it is that God is to be found and His kingdom entered by new birth. But having given this message, the message is given only in part. To complete the message Quakerism says—Here is a way. Here is a way to God. Here are practices that will lead [you] to discover God in yourself and in your fellowmen. Here are means and methods that enable you to recover the indwelling divinity and realize that you and we are part of it. Here is a life that will promote growth, transformation, new birth. Here is a way that, if followed, will lead into God, into His kingdom, his power and his glory. Now there is that of God in us. The we will be in that of God. Now God's love is in us. The we will be in that love, and we shall love God and live.

Quakerism is not unique in proclaiming that something of God is in man. Hinduism proclaims the same. Friends are not the only ones to discover that God is within man. The Catholic mystics made the same discovery. Brother Lawrence said, "He is within us; seek Him not elsewhere." Quakers are not the only ones to pray, to worship, to engage in a number of other inward practices. The inward practices of the Friends are among the root-practices of the religious life, common to all genuine ways. What is unique about our way is precisely the way in which these several elements are combined in a living whole. It is this whole that [has]

"The Message of Quakerism" (ca. 1945) is published here for the first time by permission of the Beinecke Rare Book and Manuscript Library, Yale University, New Haven, Connecticut.

no counterpart anywhere in the world. Yet its uniqueness is not the important feature. The important feature is its effectiveness. It stands or falls by the same test. Will it work for us? Can we make it work? Do we really and deeply and utterly want it to work? Do we want to point our lives Godwards? Do we want to become God-centered? Do we seek God's kingdom, His light and love, first and last and above all else? If so, our religion will serve us. And if it serves us, then and then only can we convey the conviction to others that it will serve them.

Friends, now is the time. If we delay it may be too late. The calls that came fifty years ago may have been premature. But the calls that came three years ago, and again last year, from Rufus Jones, were not premature. They were right on time. Never has there been such need. The need of light and love is greater now, if I am any image, than it was during the ministry of Jesus Christ. It is greater now than in the time of George Fox. Never has it been so great. There, on the other hand, is the immense demand. The supply is not adequate. We must do our part to make it adequate. The Society of Friends must contribute its full quota.

There is a race going on. Between education and catastrophe. Education, slow. Catastrophe, rapid. A third way—transformation—sudden mutation—that is, new birth. We must tell the world that this is possible. By our own lives and persons, we must show the world that this is possible. A quickened sense of the contemporary need should spur us. Yet the underlying motive should be, not merely to avert disaster, but to fulfill man's high destiny—to grow up to God.

The Flavor of Man

Once again we approach the spring season. Soon a new cycle of life will start in the earth; and all men, if not participants, will be beneficiaries. We advance towards new birth in the natural order. Man's hands and man's machines will be in the fields. The store of things to eat will be replenished. More generously we shall have light and warmth from the sun, and life-giving waters. The earth and all of its teeming life, man excepted, will show abundance. God shall be manifest in His World. Dawn will be the herald; and when full day comes it will come with glory.

It was this season that Nicholas Herman, known to us as Brother Lawrence, was anticipating when he saw the bare tree that soon would be renewed to full foliage, and received a high view of the providence and power of God, and felt kindled in him a true and abiding love of God. He was then eighteen years of age, having been a soldier and a footman. Thus by God's grace the former soldier became a tender person, the footman received a measure of holiness. Then and there that young man was given the flavor of man, for the primary ingredient of man's substance is love, love of God, love of man, and through love, a sense of unity with all creation.

* * *

And once again, these being the days just before things start growing, catalogues arrive from the large houses that supply seeds for the gardens

---

This speech was privately published as *The Flavor of Man* (Philadelphia: The Young Friends Movement of the Philadelphia Yearly Meeting, 1949). It is reprinted here by permission of the Philadelphia Yearly Meeting.

of America. Not long ago my wife was going through one of the catalogues that annually fascinate her, when she suddenly exclaimed, "Listen to this! Here's something for you." Indeed it was. This is what she read:

> Crystal Apple. 65 days. An amazingly attractive cucumber, perfectly round, crystal-white at all stages, with a sweetness and lack of cucumber flavor that is remarkable. Produces a tremendous number of fruit about the size of a lemon when mature.

Crystal Apple. It is not called a cucumber. It has neither the shape nor the size of a cucumber. And, to cap it all, it remarkably lacks the cucumber flavor! What ingenuity and labor went into the production of this cucumber that isn't a cucumber! Is this not typical of twentieth-century man?

Consider the bread without the flavor of bread. In any restaurant you can get milk that hardly tastes like milk. Could it be that here in Philadelphia there is water that does not taste like water? Experts have some unpleasant but important facts for us. They tell us that it is doubtful whether there is a single stream in the United States which has not deteriorated during the past hundred years. The air of our cities is becoming smog. On most farms the topsoil is depleted. Much of our work is without the flavor of creativity; our literature without the flavor of literature; our religion without the flavor of religion.

Outstanding at this time is the fact that we have peace without the flavor of peace. But the wars we wage have the full horrible flavor of war. The bombs we make are not Crystal Apples.

* * *

We in America pride ourselves on being well off. Compared to the majority in Europe and Asia we are. But compared to the full norm of mature man ours is a poor life. Whether we be materially rich or poor, most of us live in spiritual scarcity. David, the writer of the 23rd psalm, could say and virtually sing, "My cup runneth over." We cannot. Our cups are more nearly empty.

It is this inner scarcity that causes the frustration so evident in human life as ordinarily lived. It is this frustration, in turn, that sets people against people in domestic antagonisms, racial conflicts, class wars, international wars—one party wanting to punish the other for its own frustration, one hoping to wrest from the other what neither possesses.

Frustration sets people against people in strife and war. Strife and war still further bleed us. Frustration thus increases, causing ever more acute conflict. This is the vicious circle that mankind is caught in, from which we must break free. This is the locked situation that holds us tight, from which we must be liberated, from which we must arise. But how are we to rise? Not even a balloon can rise if it is empty. We must be filled. Then, as George Fox and others have demonstrated, no outside force can hold us down or prevent us from doing our share to enable others to become fulfilled.

* * *

Three hundred years ago in England there arose a people—and they did rise. They came upon a power. A power gathered them, and they knew they were related to the Divine Being. By awakening they opened, by opening there flowed into them an ample measure of human substance from their own resources, and, from the sacred Source, a goodly measure of the life that is above this life. A light, which previously had been hearsay, the light of Christ, invaded them. A love, which formerly was but a word to them, became the potent reality of their lives, the love of God. They found themselves changing, being born anew through a spiritual birth. Darkness and death fell away; and their condition ceased being that of spiritual scarcity in the midst of spiritual abundance. It became that of abundance within an immeasurably greater store.

At first they were not called Quakers, nor did they seek to become Quakers. They sought contact with the mighty power whose touch makes men tremble. They sought to be Christians through and through, to possess what they professed, to be followers of Christ and more, to have Christ and his redemptive love real to them—to know this, to *be* this, experimentally. And to this end they disciplined their total lives.

Each in his and her measure made the discovery which the whole world awaits; namely, that there are direct and immediate links between man and God; and that, when man's seeking is crowned by God's grace, the apparent separateness of man from Deity is superseded by a wondrous partnership. No other discovery can mean to us what this one means. With it, all that plagues us begins to fall away. Without it, discover what else you will, the hard knot of our darkness remains. Evil is evil only because it separates our consciousness from God. Overcome that separation and we have overcome evil. Pain is pain only because we lack realization that we are related to divinity. Problems are locked problems because of the same lack. The divisions between individuals and groups are so wide, and often so injurious, because of the same. Whoever realizes his connection with God is unlocked. In some measure he is released from his tight self to God and to men. All life is transvalued. Days and nights have sacred meanings.

Those early Friends, as we know, were gathered from all ranks and levels of society, and from all occupations. Unified into one body were farmers, fishermen, tradesmen, innkeepers, shipmasters, jailers, soldiers, blacksmiths, preachers, ladies, knights, squires. There is indication that certain thieves, harlots, and murderers were affected. Many were changed from their old ways to the new way, and what they had been was as nothing compared to what they now became.

God's radiance spread from man to man. People felt as though a holy contagion were upon them. As the word of life was spoken in each one, each became of good substance and good flavor, and all were joined together by the Spirit wherein men have brotherhood. An irresistible power was in them, behind them, before them. Knowing what was being wrought within themselves, and how swiftly, and how rapidly it was spreading, they could not doubt that God's hour was at hand; that He was coming to touch and teach His people, every one, and lift them into a new dispensation with the full flavor of the Kingdom; and that they, the people now called Friends, were God's agents to transform the world.

It is difficult for us in this secular age of mechanization and global power-politics, living under the cloud of world wars and the rumble of catastrophe, to imagine the vision that glowed in those early Friends, to feel with like conviction that God's Kingdom is coming, coming swiftly, gathering the world's people into the long-awaited resurrection. We can more readily believe that anti-Christ is upon us, empowering evil, widening the path that leads to destruction.

* * *

We must acknowledge that the world of darkness is potent and, at the present time, ominous; but it is not the only possible world. There is another Being behind and above our ordinary persons. There is another world behind and above our ordinary world. We must renew the vision of that other world. The only way to renew it is to have experiences similar to those that gave it birth. To have such experiences we must seek God who gives them. The only way to seek God is to seek God first. Deny the nayward, affirm the yeaward, be true to those stirrings and motions which He starts in us, refuse priority to all else, and be faithful to the sacred.

Many British people of those days did not like the flavor of the Quakers. To some, the Friends savored not of Christ but of Satan. Others feared that these religious radicals did have the true power of the spirit, and, having it, threatened to overturn the entrenched social and churchly orders. So they broke up their meetings, stoned and beat them, and threw them into jail. In prison the Quakers were more truly free than those who committed them. And right in the jails, amid the filth and the stench, those Children of the Light continued to radiate the Light.

The dynamic center of the Quaker movement was of course a man known as George Fox, but who once said of himself that he had a name unknown to men, a new name for the new man born within him. William Penn referred to Fox as "the first blessed and glorious instrument of this work." Penn, after Fox's death, paid him one of the finest tributes ever given man to man. Excerpts from Penn's portrait will refresh those who know them and give others a sense of the substance and flavor of George Fox.

> He was a man that God endued with a clear and wonderful depth; a discerner of others' spirits, and very much a master of his own. As to man he was an original, being no man's copy. The most aweful, living, reverent frame I ever felt or beheld, I must say, was his in prayer. He exercised no authority but over evil, and that everywhere, and in all; but with love, compassion and long-suffering. Though God had visibly clothed him with a divine preference and authority, and indeed his very presence expressed a religious majesty; yet he never abused it; but held his place in the church of God with great meekness. Having been with him for weeks and months together on divers occasions, and those of the nearest and most exercising nature, I can say I never saw him out of his place, or not a match for every service or occasion. In all things he acquitted himself like a man, yea, a strong man, a new and heavenly-minded man, and all of God Almighty's making.

Admit the excesses of George Fox, take into account those of his traits which have caught the eyes of the psychiatrists, and you still have a prodigious human being—and one, moreover, who turned men not to himself, nor to the power in him, but to God and to the power in themselves. He called men to be set free, not by themselves, not by other men, but by the Truth that illumines and liberates.

* * *

When this man was in meetings he gave his flavor to the meetings; when in the market place to the market place; when in courts to the courts; when in jails to the jails. They tried to beat him down, to break his spirit. Man's spirit, when reinforced by God's, is unbreakable. They threw him into prison after prison. But he was inwardly released. No outer restriction could constrict him. In or out of jail he declared the Truth and changed people. Wherever his body was, he remained in the power, in the pure air of the spirit.

What enabled George Fox to be what he was and to do what he did? Shall we regard him as a religious genius living on a level unattainable by us? Was he favored by God more than we can ever hope to be? Not at all; but I find that some Friends of today tend to hold one or both of these views, and thereby miss the meaning that Fox's life can and should have for us. As his own ministry declared, his experiences were of a type that we may come to have, some time in God's time, provided we do our part. There were practices he engaged in which, if known and practiced by us, will promote our rise. I have no thought that we should or could become like Fox. He was no man's copy. Neither should we be his copy, or any man's. Each of us, though bearing the common human stamp, is unique. It is a matter of levels of possible spiritual awakening and attainment.

* * *

William Penn was among those opened, raised up, and set in new motion. He too ascended and became of good substance. He too extended. And within, behind, and before him was the larger substance and motion of the world that the Quakers were creating. Having entered into a new world of the spirit, he carried the flavor of it across the ocean to the land that was to become America, and began his Holy Experiment; wherein men, on a basis of wise economy, concerned government, and in all things fair dealings with one another, were to move Godwards, were to merit the grace of new birth, so that in truth and wholly they would be changed men, new men in a total New World.

What has happened to that Holy Experiment? Has it increased and spread? Is it evident in the Market Street of the city still called the City of Brotherly Love? Does it radiate from the City Hall, on top of which stands the colossal statue of William Penn? Is there an uncommon light in the eyes of the city's people, and in their hearts a common goodwill? Has it been modified and enriched by the aspirations of other peoples and the vision of other faiths, so that it now covers the entire United States? Is this what modern America means to itself and to the world?

* * *

So many of our kinsmen are in asylums so-called, in ghettos, in concentration camps and colonies, and in some high places, critically reduced below the par of man. Does it matter that some have white bodies, some black, that some are Jews, some Gentiles, some Republicans, some Democrats? It matters that they are human. It matters that they are men and women, whatever else they are or were, but have lost the powers and the faculties proper to men and women. May God reach those beyond human reach.

* * *

Fox's phase of intensive seeking covered a period of about four years, beginning with his departure from home at the age of nineteen and culminating in his first decisive experience. It is so well known that we need not dwell on it, except to recall that throughout this stage, Fox, feeling himself a stranger in the earth, underwent all manner of trials, temptations, struggles, suffering—and some openings to the truth. Time and again his needs and problems impelled him to seek help from men. Each time he was thrown back upon himself. No one could reach him and speak to his condition. Presently he found himself in a locked situation. Then came the experience indicated in the often quoted passage, "And when all my hopes in all men were gone, so that I had nothing outwardly to help me, nor could I tell what to do; then, oh! then I heard a voice which said, 'There is one, even Christ Jesus, that can speak to thy condition': and when I heard it, my heart did leap for joy."

Most interpreters of the life of George Fox give an outstanding place to this experience, as indeed they should. Some give the impression that it was Fox's main and highest experience. To my mind, there is nothing to indicate that it was a deep rise. Not yet was he radically changed. Not yet did he extend to others, publishing the Truth. It was a rise of joy, to be sure. It marked the point where belief became a certainty and was reinforced by a higher authority. It was a turning point, without doubt. And, though not itself a transforming experience, it signaled, as we can see in retrospect, that Fox's arduous climb was soon to be graced by an effortless ascent.

* * *

Toward the end of his twenty-third year Fox began his ministry, the many forms of his apostolic work. Not yet, however, had he completely come up over. He continued under temptations and sufferings for yet a while. We can see from the context that he felt himself somewhat held down when he had the opening recorded in the memorable words, "I saw also that there was an ocean of darkness and death, but an infinite ocean of light and love which flowed over the ocean of darkness."

Presently came his second deep rise. It was without doubt a major transformation. He called it a great work of the Lord. The experience lasted for about two weeks, after which he was a risen man, a Child of the Light, so changed that even his body appeared new-moulded. He wrote: "For I had been brought through the very ocean of darkness and death, and through and over the power of Satan, by the eternal, glorious power of Christ; even through that darkness was I brought, which covered-over all the world, and which chained down all, and shut up all in death." Thereafter his extension to men increased in height, depth, breadth; and many were the convincements.

Another ascent came about two years later. It is the one which most concerns us here. His account of it begins with the arresting declaration:

> Now was I come up in spirit through the flaming sword, into the paradise of God. All things were new; and all the creation gave another smell unto me than before, beyond what words can utter. I knew nothing but pureness, and innocency, and righteousness, being renewed up into the image of God by Christ Jesus, to the state of Adam, which he was in before he fell.

On the basis of this testimony we can see that Fox had again quite risen out of the ordinary condition of man, this time into a higher condition which he recognized as a definite state, calling it the state of the unfallen Adam. Unless we have had a similar experience, we will not understand the nature of that state; but can we not sense the wonder and the fullness that would be ours were we in it? Surely it would seem enough to satisfy our aspirations. But not yet had the summit been reached. Fox goes on to say: "I was immediately taken up in spirit, to see into another or more steadfast state than Adam's in innocency, even into a state in Christ Jesus that should never fall." Though he did not say he rose into it, he realized that it is there, and attainable.

Three conditions of man! Two above the ordinary condition! As I understand it, men in the ordinary condition fulfill, at best, but one-third of their spiritual potentialities, usually less. Thus we see in a new light why spiritual scarcity prevails, and how there may be abundance. Risen to the state of the unfallen Adam, we would fulfill two-thirds of our potentialities. Only when transfigured into the state in Christ would all our potentialities be realized.

* * *

As best we could, we have lifted our eyes to the hills. It may have seemed a bit hazy up there, the view none too clear. Our sight may be unaccustomed to such gazing. But we have seen, at least in idea, that there are two conditions of life above the one that most of us are in. We have had a glimpse of the stretch to the human summit—at which point man becomes more than man, he partakes of the divine. How do we feel? Are we encouraged or discouraged, challenged or overborne?

We may be sure that George Fox, writing of his transcending experiences, did so with the aim of pointing man to his true destiny and giving substance to man's hopes. We may be as sure that Rufus Jones and Thomas Kelly, in our day, wrote and spoke as they did with a similar aim. Yet many of us, on being shown the high vistas, feel not uplifted but downcast, even futile.

* * *

We have seen how Brother Lawrence was enabled, and George Fox. Rufus Jones recorded at least one of his higher enabling experiences, as did Thomas Kelly. One came to Antoine de Saint-Exupery while piloting an airplane over enemy territory; one to Starr Daly while in prison. The list is longer than we may think. Dante, William Blake, Thoreau, Emerson, Walt Whitman. . . . It includes not only those known through their written records, but a large number unrecorded. Are we left out? For the time being, perhaps; but not forever. If we do our part, then, in God's own time, there shall happen even to the least of His children all that has happened to the greatest. On this faith I stand. Let us stand together.

* * *

In the human life of this era it is still possible to ascend and extend. In the America of today there are hills that for us can be Pendle Hills, if we are risen within ourselves. On earth there are more people than ever before, beset by more problems and a greater danger. We need, more than ever, that some seekers shall find, shall receive the light and love that liberates us from our ego-prisons, and works a resurrection. And it will happen, if God so wills. In our day some people somewhere shall be born of God, and become agents of the Power, and form with one another a loving body to cherish the life and share it with mankind.

Man, if he so wills, can do much for man, but only in the natural and human orders. We can be men only if we help each other. God alone can lift man into His order, and impart the substance of the divine. To want less than this is to miss the high purpose of religion; is, for Friends, to disavow the origin and aim of their own testimonies; is, for any and every man, to consign himself to the welter of evils and conflicts which can never be resolved save as we emerge from scarcity by receiving life from the sacred source within ourselves. We must advance towards new birth in the divine-human order.

May it come to pass through our struggles, our sufferings and joys, the little acts of service, the greater acts of heroism, our daily work, our devotions, our tragedies and triumphs . . . God grow us to Thee.

Bibliography

Published Essays by Jean Toomer

"Authority, Inner and Outer." *Friends Intelligencer* 104 (1947): 352–53.

"Blessing and Curse." *Friends Intelligencer* 107 (1950): 576–77.

"The Critic of Waldo Frank: Criticism, An Art Form." *S4N*, 30 (Jan. 1924): n.p.

"The Hill." In *America and Alfred Stieglitz: A Collective Portrait*, edited by Waldo Frank, Lewis Mumford, Dorothy Norman, Paul Rosenfeld, and Harold Rugg. Garden City, New York: The Literary Guild, 1934. 295–302.

"Keep the Inward Watch." *Friends Intelligencer* 102 (1945): 411–12.

"Letter from America." Published as "Lettre D'Amerique," translated into French by Victor Llona. *Bifur* 1 (May 1929): 105–19.

"Meditations: Evil." *New Mexico Literary Sentinel*, Sept. 7, 1937, 8.

"Meditations: From a Farm." *New Mexico Literary Sentinel*, Aug. 31, 1937, 8.

"Meditations: JT and PB; Make Good." *New Mexico Literary Sentinel*, July 20, 1937, 6, 7.

"A New Force for Co-operation." *Adelphi* 9 (Oct. 1934): 25–31.

"Notations on *The Captain's Doll*." *Broom* 5 (Aug. 1923): 47–49.

"Open Letter to Gorham Munson." *S4N* 25 (Mar. 1923): n.p.

"The Other Invasion." *Friends Intelligencer* 101 (1944): 423–24.

"Oxen Cart and Warfare." *The Little Review* X (Autumn-Winter 1924-25): 44–48.

"The Presence of Love." *Friends Intelligencer* 101 (1944): 771–72.

"Race Problems and Modern Society." In *Problems of Civilization*, edited by Baker Brownell. New York: Van Nostrand, 1929. 67–111.

Review of Zona Gale's *Faint Perfume*. *Broom* 5 (Oct. 1923): 180–81.

"Santa Claus Will Not Bring Peace." *Friends Intelligencer* 100 (1943): 851–52.

"Something More." *Friends Intelligencer* 107 (1950): 164–65.

"Spiritual Scarcity." *Philadelphia Inquirer,* Mar. 28, 1949, 6–7.
"The Uncommon Man." *Friends Intelligencer* 103 (1946): 147–48.
"These Three." *Friends Intelligencer* 100 (1943): 647–48.
"Today May We Do It." *Friends Intelligencer* 102 (1945): 19–20.
"Waldo Frank's *Holiday.*" *Dial* 75 (Oct. 1923): 383–86.
"Worship and Love." *Friends Intelligencer* 103 (1946): 695–96.

Major Unpublished Essays by Jean Toomer

"Book of Aims." 1938. Jean Toomer Collection, Beinecke Rare Book and Manuscript Library, Yale University, New Haven, Connecticut (hereafter referred to as JTC).
"The Crock of Problems." 1928. JTC.
"The Message of Quakerism." Ca. 1945. JTC.
"The Negro Emergent." 1924. JTC.
"Negro Psychology in *The Emperor Jones.*" 1921. JTC.
"Opinions on the Questions of the *Cahiers de l'Etoile.*" 1929. JTC.
"Paul Rosenfeld in Port." 1924. JTC.
"Psychologic Papers." 1937. JTC.
"The Psychology and Craft of Writing." Ca. 1930. JTC.
Review of Richard Aldington's "The Art of Poetry." 1921. JTC.
"The South in Literature." 1923. JTC.
"Talks With Peter." 1937. JTC.
"Values and Fictions: A Psychological Record." 1925. JTC.
"Why I Entered the Gurdjieff Work." 1941. JTC.
"Why I Joined the Society of Friends." 1941. JTC.

Published Monographs by Jean Toomer

A Fiction and Some Facts. Mill House Pamphlets. Doylestown, Pa., n.d.